Fishing for Praise

Fishing for Praise

Aspects of Praise

PAUL POULTON

RESOURCE *Publications* • Eugene, Oregon

FISHING FOR PRAISE
Aspects of Praise

Copyright © 2008 Paul Poulton. All rights reserved. Except for brief quotations in critical publications or reviews, no part of this book may be reproduced in any manner without prior written permission from the publisher. Write: Permissions, Wipf and Stock, 199 W. 8th Ave., Eugene, OR 97401.

ISBN 13: 978-1-55635-495-3

Manufactured in the U.S.A.

Unless otherwise indicated, Scripture quotations are from the Holy Bible, New International Version Copyright © 1973, 1978, 1984 by the International Bible Society.

*Big thanks to Nancy Shoptaw,
copyeditor extraordinaire,
and also to Lorraine Poulton,
and staff at Wipf and Stock.*

Contents

1. Fishing for Praise / 1
2. Tacked on Praise / 7
3. Common Praise / 11
4. Public Praise / 20
5. Corporate Praise / 30
6. Misplaced Praise / 42
7. A Life of Praise / 60
8. Creative Praise / 74
9. The Shape of Praise / 98

   Bibliography / 101

I

Fishing for Praise

Praise is a normal part of life; we see it in lots of places if we care to look. What Christians do in church isn't odd; it fits into life, as we know it.

Some people, deists as they are called (there are a lot of them about, although they may not be aware of their name), wonder why we have to praise God. "Can't we believe in Him without having to adore and praise Him," they ask? Or, "Surely God doesn't need our praise!" Benjamin Franklin, himself a deist, said, "I cannot conceive otherwise than that He, the Infinite Father, expects or requires no worship or praise from us, but that He is even infinitely above it."[1]

The Bible tends to disagree with Benjamin Franklin, though it is fair to say that *God* doesn't need our praise. But is it *we* who need to praise Him?

God has no needs; we have plenty, and one of them is our need to praise. For us to be completely human, made in God's image as He intended us to be, praise ought to be a part of our life. Praise has an important role in the framework that makes us human. But it is a need that some people are hesitant to admit. An alien from outer space would be forgiven for thinking it is humans who need the praise. We love to receive it but are sometimes reluctant to give it.

The Bible says, "Let another praise you, and not your own mouth" (Prov 27:2). So let's get this out of the way at

1. Franklin, *"Articles of Belief and Acts of Religion,"* lines 18–20.

the outset—don't blow your own trumpet and don't fish for compliments. If you do, most people will recognize what you're up to because most of us have done it ourselves. We think we're skilled anglers, deft at catching praise for ourselves as we learn how to nudge the conversation in the right direction. We're fishermen who know how to land a big one straight from the complimentary pool. We might as well sing the old melody, "I will have a fishy on my little dishy, when the boat comes in." And when the boat does come in, when I get the compliment I was looking for, there will be many drooling mouths wanting a bit of my fish on their little dish. I'll be like a film star at the Oscar's, saying it wouldn't have been possible without the director. I must give credit to the writers and praise my supporting cast. In fact, by the time I've finished slicing up my glorious fish, there will hardly be any of the original compliment left for me. I'll be left telling other people just how big my fish was and they'll think, "Oh yeah, another fisherman's tale."

There is an important lesson to be learned: Don't go fishing for compliments; let them come in their own good time. "Modesty is the only sure bait when you angle for praise," said The Earl of Chesterfield.[2] The Lord is able to prepare a table for you in the presence of your enemies (Ps 23:5). He will fill your table so full of food that you will say, "No more Lord, please, I'm full up." Just as He fed the 5000, there were a lot of satisfied people. Twelve basketfuls of fish and bread remained (Matt 14:20–21). That is God's heart; He loves to give.

When you are patient, praise will come your way from the most unexpected source and it will come just when your enemies have turned up to see it. Jesus was in Simon the Leper's house when a woman arrived and poured very expensive perfume on His head. The enemies of Christ

2. Chesterfield, *"Lord Chesterfield's Letters,"* letter CXIII.

couldn't stand the waste and rebuked her harshly, but Jesus said she had done a beautiful thing (Mark 14:3–6). When the righteous man is exalted, the wicked will see it and be vexed (Ps 112:9–10).

Jesus said some people love praise from men rather than praise from God (John 12:43). He also implored believers to make an effort to obtain the praise that comes from God (John 5:44). Praise is intrinsic to God's being, which is why we need to praise if we are made in His image. Praise comes from God; it flows from Him. He is an encourager. He loves to strengthen and inspire us. He is a Father who loves to build up His children. He is a manager who longs to say, "Well done, good and faithful servant." God is more than willing to praise us! This praise thing is reciprocal. God wants to praise us, and if we are praiseworthy, He will.

People will get to hear His praise, too. When Jesus stood in the Jordan River with a crowd gathered around, God the Father proclaimed—for all to hear—that this was His Son in whom He was well pleased (Matt 3:17). The more we become like Jesus, the more we are pleasing to God, and God has a way of making sure people know this—without any help from us. In fact, if we try to let people know ourselves, we cancel out any credit we may have gained. How can we be like Jesus when we go around boasting about how great we are? He said, "Learn from me, for I am gentle and humble in heart" (Matt 11:29).

Children shout about their achievements and we tolerate it, but as they get older, we encourage them to stop doing it. Children who grow up loving their own reflection should prepare themselves for a lonely old age. Yet, God commands us to praise Him (Ps 150). We are told to ascribe to Him the glory due to His name (Ps 29:2), and to bless Him (Ps 34:1). And all this praise should not be done in a discreet manner but with a shout (Ps 33:3) and a loud noise so that any onlookers can't mistake what's going on. To make matters worse, we are not only told to do all that, but to do it at all times in all places (Ps 34:1). Hence those who follow His advice sing praise at weddings, funerals, concert halls, in church, at work, on the radio, in prison—even as they are burned alive at the stake.

To the skeptic, this is a very irritating command. If one thing is guaranteed to generate a few enemies, it is giving God credit in general conversation. But don't fret, God will see to it that you get praised in return and the skeptic will be there to see it. The man in the street may ask if there is nowhere in heaven or on earth where he can flee from this presence that demands our praise? Is nowhere sacred? Why couldn't the good Lord above be a little more like us humans and temper His appetite for praise with a pinch of guile, a smattering of deceit, and a bit of angling? We seem to do so well at it, couldn't He? But surely, the unbeliever is misled. His questioning is not good. He errs, not knowing the Scriptures or He who inspired them. God is not a child that He should stamp His foot, cry out, and demand our attention. As the deists say, why should He want our praise; we, who are lower than the angels, lower even than the first estate in which we were created? We have been corrupted. We miss the mark, and have become brute beasts that devour one another. What kind of value does our praise have on it anyway?

Imagine a young man who writes a poem and decides to read it to his partially deaf aunt. Upon hearing it she tells her nephew that he will be the next poet laureate, better even than William Wordsworth. The young man would be ill advised to leave full-time employment to take up poetry because of his aunt's praise and enthusiasm. He actually needs admiration from a publisher who knows talent when he sees it.

Or, imagine a young girl who fancies herself a pop star as she sings daily into her bedroom mirror using a hairbrush for a microphone. Everyone in the house runs for cover and shuts doors when she starts—except for her dog, which makes himself comfy and howls his approval.

We are the deaf aunt and the howling dog. Look at God's creative work. We didn't design trees; we would never have thought of them. They are God's handiwork, His artwork. They are pleasing to the eye; they serve a useful purpose. They are, in fact, excellent. God knows all this already: He looked around and saw that "it was good" (Gen 1:10, 12, 18, 21, 25). God who created and shaped protons, neutrons, electrons, and quarks doesn't need us to tell Him He made a good job of the universe. It took us thousands of years to even realize atoms were here. Yet God, knowing all this, still seeks us out and bids us to come and worship. What a privilege! It is like the frog being asked to kiss the princess.

Praise is all around us; we hear it often and in many places. The teacher praises the pupil whose essay achieves good marks, the lover praises his beloved on her resplendent appearance, and the parent praises the child for good behavior.

We praise footballers, hairdressers, and chefs. We even praise our dogs when they go and wait by the door rather than leaving a puddle by the couch. Praise is a part of life and usually appears in the happier moments: when a goal has been scored, when we leave the hairdresser's looking good, or are pleasantly full after an evening meal.

A few moments ago, a boy I had never met before knocked on my door and asked if he could clean my car. Now I look out the window and see that he is doing a good job. He has saved me some work and given me more time to write this book. So, when I pay him I will probably praise him by saying, "Good job Matthew, well done." We praise because we are pleased, we are pleased because someone gives us pleasure, and someone gives us pleasure because they excel at something; they are doing something well that we enjoy.

Here we reach an important point: God does all things well. When He asks us to praise Him, He is asking us to enjoy Him, to delight in Him, in what He has made, in what He has done, and to be glad that what He has made is good because He is good. Isn't that the first statement of the *Shorter Catechism*? "What is the chief end of man? Man's chief end is to glorify God and to enjoy Him for ever."[3] We need to praise. The person who can't praise—we've all met them—can't enjoy. That leaves half of person. A human being who can't enjoy him or herself is a sad person. Some people can't praise anything or anyone. They have an aversion to saying good things about other people. They may go through the motions of enjoying themselves—we've seen the man who wants to get drunk and may seem like he's enjoying himself, but can't even say anything good about the beer he's drinking. Perhaps he complains about the price of it, or its texture, or how it used to be far better in the good old days. He is not actually enjoying it; he is vacant and trying to fill a hole. Trying to pry praise out of some people is like trying to pry open a vacuum-packed meat product with nothing but your fingers; it's well nigh impossible. If we are unwilling to praise anything, not just God, we lose some of our humanity. God loves to praise. He's an encourager. If we are made in His image, we need to praise and encourage also.

---

3. Bible Presbyterian Church Online, *Westminster Shorter Catechism*, lines 1–2.

2

Tacked on Praise

Praise isn't an appendage stuck on as a nice afterthought. It is the consummation of the event itself.

A playwright may sleeplessly wait for the morning papers after the first night's performance. If praise from the critics is forthcoming he will sleep, because months of work are now complete. He writes for the enjoyment of others and if they fail to enjoy his writing, then his work has been in vain. Critics are not always right, of course, but it won't do his play any harm to have them on board. If the audience praises his play to their friends, then the work is truly complete. Word of mouth is good publicity, and great praise.

Enjoyment is the antecedent of praise. If we enjoy ourselves, our willingness to praise the source of our enjoyment increases. God's presence fills us with joy (Ps 16:11). If we could catch one small glimpse of Jesus in all His heavenly brilliance, we could do nothing else but praise Him. The meekness of the Lamb would call to us in all its urgency—who could stop his heart crying out with the psalmist, "You are the most excellent of men and your lips have been anointed with grace" (Ps 45:2)? While Jesus walked the earth, men were amazed at the gracious words that came from His lips (Luke 4:22). The compassion we feel when we see a child at the mercy of a wicked adult mirrors the compassion we would feel at one glimpse of the Lamb of God. One who is truly meek, mild, despised, and rejected by men, the "Man of Sorrows" (Isa 53:3) whose gentleness is evident to all, whose love radiates towards us like the sun's light. Every ounce of justice within us would cry out that this man deserves praise. Similarly, the awe we would feel seeing a lion—king of the jungle—in its natural habitat would be a small taste of the overwhelming reverence we would experience at the sight of the Lion of the tribe of Judah. Our hearts would tell us that this man deserves to be heard and revered.

Suppose for a moment that you were once trapped at work in a burning office building. Fortunately, Jack, who worked on the floor below, heard your cry for help. Postponing his own escape, he sets about the task of rescuing you. He finally lowers you to safety though he is suffering from smoke inhalation. Both of you are rushed to hospital where, after treatment, you each recover. Several years later, new employees begin work at the rebuilt premises and because Jack has decided not to confront the board of directors on a particular issue, accusations that Jack is a coward start to circulate around the office. What feelings would rise up within you if you heard this office gossip? Whatever Jack may be, he's not a coward. He must have good reasons for not talking to the directors over the issue in question. Would you hesitate to let these Johnny-come-latelies know that Jack saved your life at the risk of losing his own? If we fail to speak up for Jack, it is we who are the coward. Jack's praise needs to be heard; there is a time to speak—and this is it.

Once we realize who Christ is and what He has done, something cries out within us, "Let Him be praised!" Part of the act of seeing Christ is to cry out in praise. Jesus spoke of the *rivers of living water* that would rise up from within us (John 7:38), pushed up like a hot geyser by the pressure of the Holy Spirit who is on earth to glorify Jesus. That is why Christians have to speak of Christ and let it be known that

He is worthy to receive praise. That is why our hearts burn within us. If we know Christ, we cannot help but praise Him, one glimpse is all it takes. But sometimes our eyes are clouded, we can't see. A light from heaven shone on Saul, a Pharisee who had spent time studying the Scriptures yet failed to see. A voice from heaven spoke to him and Saul's response was, "Who are you Lord" (Acts 9:5)? All those years of reading the Scriptures and he didn't even know who the Lord was. He was blind for three days, yet during his period of darkness could see more clearly than he had ever seen. Saul saw one fleeting glimpse of Christ in His glory and that was all it took.

The soldier at the crucifixion looked at Jesus as He died and said, "Truly this man was the Son of God" (Mark 15:39). Peter protested, "Depart from me for I am a sinful man" (Luke 5:8), which was Peter's praise, indicating that he was bad but Jesus was good. Blind Bartimaeus cried out with a loud voice, "Jesus, Son of David have mercy on me" (Mark 10:47). The people near him told him to shut up, so he shouted even louder. Something awakened his heart; he'd been touched by the otherworldly fragrance of hope and now the intoxicating flavor of faith was in his heart. He proclaimed that Jesus was in fact the Son of David, and he was healed.

Scripture refers to leaping, dancing, and praising God (Acts 3:8; Ps 149:3). To know God is to enjoy Him; to enjoy Him is to praise Him. If we do not praise God, we must question whether we have ever had a divine glimpse of who He really is. The Scripture does not say in vain, "Taste and see that the Lord is good" (Ps 34:8). John the Baptist said, "He must increase and I must decrease" (John 3:30). If we resist the temptation to be self-publicists and follow John's desire to promote Christ, we move away from being dysfunctional humans and closer to the glorified beings we will one day be in heaven.

A car is made to run on fuel, although it is possible to move the car without it. You could, for instance, ask a few friends to help you push it. You could even roll it down a hill quite easily. But no one in his right mind would expect his friends to push his car every time he wants to take a journey. Our lives are made to praise God. If we don't do that, we may roll along for a while and even go down some descents where life seems easy, but our spiritual engine is never ignited. Like the car without fuel is the person whose heart has never glimpsed Christ.

3

Common Praise

When we've been there ten thousand years
Bright shining as the sun
We've no less days to sing God's praise
Than when we first begun.

WHEN I was a boy these thoughts didn't fill me with the same excitement they seemed to fill the hymnwriter with when he wrote them. I noticed that in church people sang this verse with added gusto as though praising God forever and ever was a good thing. This was hard to understand: sitting motionless in church for a long service and hearing that our full-time occupation in heaven would be singing hymns to God. It sort of filled me with a certain glumness and despondency that took some while to shake off.

When the six-day war broke out in 1967, I was told that this was one of the last signs to be fulfilled before Christ's second coming, that His return and our being caught up to heaven was imminent, even at the very door. As I walked along the street that day, I felt like the drowning man whose life flashes before his eyes. I knew my parents would be with me in heaven but what about Jackie, my girlfriend at school? I remember thinking that our relationship was useless because I was a "goner." It seemed to me that becoming my girlfriend was futile because as soon as we had got to know each other, I'd be whisked up into that big church in the sky whereupon I'd be singing slow hymns forever and ever accompanied by an organ the size of Mount Everest. The thought had escaped me that some people actually like slow hymns, and if such a heaven existed as I supposed, then to them it really would be heaven—slow hymn heaven. Well, the Second Coming, as you may be aware, didn't happen. Neither did my relationship with Jackie, but I now think I understand heaven a little better.

What people enjoy varies immensely, depending upon age, sex, energy levels, culture, personal taste, etc. Different people enjoy different pursuits and what people enjoy, they generally praise—if they can praise at all. In fact, the enjoyment has not really run its full course until we have praised the object of our enjoyment. How often do we hear remarks like "Hey, did you see that film last night?" or "You missed a great game on Saturday!" Irish Comedian Dave Allen used to tell a joke about a Catholic priest who shot a round of golf early one Sunday morning when he should have been about his priestly duties. God decided to punish him by giving him a hole-in-one. When St. Peter asked how a hole-in-one could be perceived as punishment, the Lord said, "But whom can he tell?"

When we experience enjoyment, we begin to ache with the load of pleasure we are carrying and must get someone to help us bear it. Jeremiah said, "If I say in my heart 'I will not mention Him or speak any more in His name' His word is in my heart like a burning fire, shut up in my bones. I am weary of holding it in; indeed, I cannot" (Jer 20:9). From the song, "Sweet Sweet Song of Salvation," Larry Norman sang, "When you know a pretty story you don't let it go unsaid."

Think of a young man who is secretly in love with a girl, so secret, not even the girl knows it. His love moves him to write a song about her. At "open mic" night he gets a chance to sing it while she is in the audience. Most people seem to like the song for its depth of feeling. Afterwards people begin telling him how much they enjoyed his song. The girl too is one of the people moved by the sincerity of the lyrics. The young man plucks up his courage and tells the girl that it was she who inspired the song. She receives the compliment well and they begin to see more of each other. Notice what happened to the lover. He enjoyed seeing the girl, and then enjoyed writing the song that praised the girl, enjoyed singing the song, and finally enjoyed seeing more of the girl. It's a cycle: Pleasure results in praise, which is pleasurable in itself, therefore breeding more praise. Heaven will be both pleasure and praise.

At God's right hand, says the Bible, are pleasures forevermore (Ps 16:11). We will feast on the abundance of His house and drink from His river of delights (Ps 36:8), which will result in the pleasure of an uninhibited ability to express praise. It is here we get closer to a true picture of heaven—much more so than my boyhood slow-hymns-going-on-forever theory. God has created many pleasures; there are many aspects to *pleasure* as there are many aspects of *praise*. One aspect of praise is to say that God is good, a second is to praise Him for something good He has done, and yet another is to praise Him for the good things He is going to do.

Heaven will not be a monotonous unrelenting hymn rendition, but an inexorable multiplicity of pleasures that, in turn, give rise to just as many aspects of praise. The worthier the recipient, the greater delight in praising. As we discover through the eons of eternity more wondrous aspects of the divine goodness, so will our pleasure be even greater. The further into heaven we explore, the more there is to discover; the deeper we go, the deeper it gets. Like in the Narnia stories, "Further up and further in,"[1] and the further they went the more they realized how much further there

---

1. Lewis, *The Last Battle*, 163.

was to explore. Heaven is an exciting place to be. Everyone will have something to offer. We will all reflect some amazing aspect of the divine glory.

Here on earth, some people sap our time. We always seem to be giving to them without receiving anything from them in return. Not so in heaven. The weakest saint here on earth will be transformed into a being filled with speed, strength, and dynamism in heaven. What some people consider to be the most boring Christian here on earth will be changed into a fascinating, interesting, and absorbing individual. So much so that if they appeared this way on earth they would never be left alone by others trying to see them, phone them, text them, and generally be close to them. In heaven, everyone will have something of value to offer, and God will be praised for the way some aspect of His radiance is reflected in each one of us.

Neither should we fear losing our individuality in heaven. We won't be absorbed by God, as some religions teach. No, the Bible teaches that we will have work to do, positions of authority to fill. Each one of us is uniquely made so that we resonate some vista of the eternal God. The more like God we become, the more we become our true selves. The further away from God we get, the more we lose of our essence, until some ultimately lose their souls completely. We can see the beginnings of it here on earth if we look closely. For what we are on earth is a microcosm of what we will be. Each of us have something unique to offer, a talent that no one else has in the same way that we do. For example, someone may be musical, but they are not musical in exactly the same way as anyone else. Another may be artistic but they are not artistic in exactly the same way as anyone else, or a good teacher, or writer, or any of the innumerable talents that God has placed with people. We all add our own flavor to whatever it is that God has given us as our personal gift.

I spoke at the funeral of Harry, a friend who had learning disabilities, and as I gave the tribute it became apparent that Harry had his own job to do here on earth. He was a unique blend of color in the spectrum of life; he had his own message to carry to those around him. Harry made us stop and think and remember that life is not about the endless pursuit of wealth but that we need to take time with people. Being with Harry in some way helped me to remember who God is and who we are.

Of course some people don't live up to their full potential, some never even explore any of their potential. Hell breeds monotonous emptiness. It is there that the empty words of the flatterer become known for what they are. The servile, the fawning, those who ingratiated themselves to further their own profile, those who had no genuine feeling in their expressions of praise, but rather used praise to further their own selfish ends. Those will also be there who are unworthy recipients of praise. "Do not," says the proverb, "Eat the food of a stingy man, you will vomit up the little that you have eaten and will have wasted your compliments" (Prov 23:6).

When praise is given to the undeserving, the glory offered them passes straight through them, having no reality on which to attach it self. The light shone in their direction cannot be seen, having no reflective surface on which to bounce back to the eyes of others. They are a black hole from which even light cannot be returned, their avaricious greed sucking in anything that passes nearby. Fellow creatures won't be able to see them; they disappear from view into their own darkness. To remain human, they desperately need to give something out, but they have become what they are. "The tree has fallen so shall it lie" (Eccl 11:3), all that remains is the residue of a human being. No crowns of glory can sit on their heads, for there is no substance on which the crown can sit. But, more of that in a later chapter.

The subject of praise can give us a certain amount of insight into heaven and hell, but what of earth? We know what God is like from what He has made. There have been men in every age of earth's history that have spotted God's glory in the common events of life. Towards the end of Malcolm Muggeridge's life, the well-known British journalist, satirist, soldier-spy, and Christian apologist said, "For every situation and eventuality there is a parable if you look carefully enough."[2] In the parabolic story *The Lion the Witch and the Wardrobe*, the children entered a common wardrobe but found it uncommonly supernatural. Its author, C. S. Lewis, was showing us something. Joshua saw the walls of Jericho, David saw a small stone, and Gideon saw a torch and clay jar. Locked into the universe is the hidden code that, once broken, opens the door to see glimpses of heaven here on earth.

Sir Isaac Newton regarded the entire universe as a cryptogram. Newton, an English physicist and mathematician and the greatest scientist of his era, thought the cryptogram, or coded message, was set by the Almighty.[3] Romans 1:19–20 says, "What may be known about God is plain . . . God's invisible qualities—His eternal power and divine nature—have been clearly seen, being understood from what has been made." Ordinary life as we live it reveals God, if we care to look. Interwoven into space-time are doors that once opened, reveal a glimpse of heaven here on earth. (Heaven is not as far away as popular myth tries to tell us it is.) Horatius Bonar spotted the code and wrote the hymn:

> Praise in the common things of life
> its goings out and in;
> Praise in each duty and each deed
> however small and mean.
> So shall no part of day or night

2. Muggeridge, *Conversion—A Spiritual Journey*, 23.
3. Keynes, *Newton, the Man*, 310.

> from sacredness be free;
> but all my life, in every step,
> be fellowship with Thee.

God loves to communicate to us, and He does it artistically and evocatively with enthusiasm, flair, and panache. We, ourselves, talk about the *art of conversation*. Communication is an art and God excels at it. What excellent poetry we find in Psalm chapter 1. The first verse includes the words "walk," "stand," and "sit" to make its point, giving the reader the feeling of progression. These are lyrics in which a lot of thought has been given. There is an important message in this Psalm, and God helps us to understand it by using phrases that are rhythmical and poetic. They evoke pictures in our mind that are helpful in understanding its message. God speaks to us through poetry; the Holy Spirit is a poet. Zephaniah 3:17 tells us that the Lord will rejoice over us with singing; the Father is a singer. Jesus alludes to Himself trying to make the people dance by playing the flute in Matthew 11:17. Embedded in the fabric of the universe are messages from God. He is trying to reach us anyway He can. He has given us a heart that responds to art, music, and poetry.

People travel some distance to attend a concert to listen to a band they enjoy, gladly spend money on the latest hardback book of a favorite author, or take time to stand in a shopping area and watch a street mime artist perform. The artist enjoys the creativity of communication and the audience enjoys being on the receiving end. Even animals communicate. The wolf will howl to rally his pack together, the pigeon will coo and strut to attract the female's attention, and a worker bee will dance in the hive to communicate the location of some newly found flowers. The dance of atoms around us that we call "space-time" is communicating something to us—if we have eyes to see.

Through the ages, one eternal purpose runs. Charles Haddon Spurgeon (1834–92), England's best-known preacher for most of the second half of the nineteenth century, said, "This is the grand design of providence, and the end to which all events must tend."[4] All events are working together, and when we begin to see the beauty of the dance and the skill of the choreographer, our hearts will soar with praise. It will dawn on us that we are not only part of the audience but also part of the dance. Jeremiah thought it prudent to remain silent for reasons of personal safety, but he found he couldn't, saying that God's words burned within him, forcing him to cry out with a powerful voice to his contemporaries. He wanted to remain an onlooker but found he was part of the play. "The Lord works out everything for His own ends—even the wicked for the day of disaster" (Prov 16:4).

Our journey through space-time is like a trip through a safari park. Space-time is a single unit and we are spirits moving through it. Space-time can be thought of as an environment for the human spirit. Our body is part of it, but our spirit is not. Our body may be here on earth but our spirit is one with Christ. So we move through it like intrepid explorers. At every turn there is something to see. Check out the ferocious lions, look at the powerful bears, or gaze at the gentle deer. Sometimes life is like being in the lion's den; it gets ferocious out there. It certainly did for Daniel. He obeyed God rather than men and continued praying—with his windows open wide—even though the king forbade it (Dan 6:10).

Life is sometimes like facing powerful bears. As a massive army headed his way, King Jehoshaphat chose leaders of his tiny army and appointed them to sing praises to the Lord, which proved to be a battle winning strategy (2 Chr

---

4. Spurgeon, *Spurgeon's Devotional Bible*.

20:21–22). Our experience of life is also sometimes like watching graceful deer. Elisha said, "Bring me a harpist," and while music filled the air, the prophet would prophesy (2 Kgs 3:15). Life is a dance; the man who knows God will join in the dance of life at all its extremities using every situation to praise the Lord. Seeing the praiseworthiness of all our circumstances means we have joy through our circumstances, and even though we are on earth, we can enjoy sitting with Christ in heavenly places. In the words of Cardinal J. H. Newman:

> God has created me to do some definite service: He has committed some work to me which He has not committed to another . . . I am a link in a chain, a bond of connection between persons. He has not created me for naught. I shall do good, I shall do His work . . . therefore I will trust Him. Whatever, wherever I am I can never be thrown away. If I am in sickness, my sickness may serve Him, in perplexity, my perplexity may serve Him, in sorrow, my sorrow may serve Him. He does nothing in vain. He knows what He is about. He may take away my friends, He may throw me among strangers. He may make me feel desolate, make my spirits sink, hide my future from me—still He knows what He is about.[5]

---

5. Newman, *Meditations and Devotions*, 1848.

4

Public Praise

SOME PEOPLE say the clothes we wear reflect our personality. Yes, I can see some truth in that—the artist is reflected in his art. God's creation reveals something about God. As Romans 1:20 says, "Ever since God created the world, His invisible qualities, His eternal power, and His divine nature have been clearly seen; they are perceived in the things God has made."

Plato explained space-time by imagining himself standing with a group of people at the opening of a large cave. All the people had their backs to the light and were facing the rear wall of the cave. They could see their shadows cast upon the rear wall and the shadows of any trees or bushes that were close to the opening of the cave. If the people moved, their shadows would move. If they stood still, so would their shadows. They could see the rough outline of what everyone was doing but couldn't see any detail; they couldn't see what a person looked like. They could tell if a person was tall or small, fat or thin. They saw profiles but no detailed representation of reality. If, however a man facing the rear wall turned his head and looked around, he would see the objects making the shadows, he would see people, and outside he would see the big wide world.[1]

The Bible teaches something remarkably similar: "We look through a glass darkly" (1 Cor 13:12 KJV). "These are

1. Plato, *Great Dialogues of Plato*, 317.

a shadow of things to come" (Col 2:17). We are told in the enigmatic Song Of Songs that someday the "Shadows will flee away" (Songs 2:17, 4:6). Every shadow here on earth is made by something; similarly every part of space-time represents something. Psalm 19:1 says, "The heavens declare the glory of God." When writers of the Old Testament spoke of "heaven and earth," they usually meant that heaven was the clouds, sky, and stars, and the earth was the world we live in. We don't often use the words "heaven and earth" today because the term "the universe" covers them both. Jesus spoke of our Father who was in heaven, not meaning that God resides particularly in the clouds or outer space. No, He saw the natural heavens as a symbol or shadow of the true spiritual heaven. Our physical heavens—the beautiful sunsets, clouds, and galaxies—are made up of physical material and photons. They declare the glory of God—they are not the glory itself—but only tell the story; they represent the glory. Pantheists mistake the shadows for the reality, believing that God and the universe are identical. One day heaven and earth will pass away (Ps 102:25–26), as all shadows pass. Until then, they speak, and there is no language where their voice is not heard (Ps 19:3).

We live in a mechanical universe; we perform mechanical acts. This is the nature of the physical dimension God has deemed that we live in. Scripture tells us not to look at those things we see but to look at the things we cannot see (2 Cor 4:18). Actions, events, and objects in this material world seem to represent something unseen. Nature itself is speaking to us, if only we could hear it. Cardinal Newman said, "Nature is a parable."[2] Using Newman's words, Malcolm Muggeridge responded, saying, "Nature is speaking to us. It is a parable of life itself, a revelation of fearful symmetry .

---

2. Newman, *Apologia pro Vita Sua*, 128.

. . ."[3] The Bible concurs with this view: The Hebrew word for "spirit" is "*ruach,*" the same word used for "breath" or "wind." The Old Testament was written in Hebrew. The New Testament was written in Greek and the Greek word for "spirit" is "*pneuma,*" which denotes "wind" or "breath," and forms the English words "pneumatic," which means "operated by air," and "pneumonia," a disease of our air-breathing lungs. God is Spirit (John 4:24), not meaning that God is the gas that surrounds planet earth; our physical air is a shadow of spirit.

In the beginning God breathed into man the breath of life, but God does not breathe; He doesn't need air to sustain His being. He is something other than the gaseous collection of atoms and molecules that make up the air around us. There is something of spirit within human beings that is put there by God. He deposited something in the core of our being that connects us to the unseen spiritual environment and this is represented by the air we breathe. We don't read of God breathing into the nostrils of animals; man alone has been made in the image of God. Air or wind is a parallel or symbol to help us learn something important. The Holy Spirit came to earth with the sound of a mighty rushing wind on the day of Pentecost. The apostles indicated that God's Spirit was now inside them, by using the air in their lungs to speak in tongues as the Spirit enabled them. As there were flames above the heads of the apostles, so God's Spirit ignites our spirit making us one with God—just as one burning piece of material can set a whole host of other things on fire. It is because His Spirit dwells in each Christian that we are one with each other.

We see the spiritual parallel of the physical world everywhere we look. Isaac Newton's cryptogram—coded world—begins to unravel. When we tell our girlfriend we

---

3. Muggeridge, "Nature is a Parable," 1614.

love her with all our heart she knows we don't mean we love her with all our blood-pump. Our physical heart represents something else at the core of our being, which we cannot see because it is immaterial. Jesus said that it matters not what type of food we eat because the food does not enter the heart (Mark 7:18–19). Here he draws a distinction between our physical heart and our spiritual heart, for food we eat does certainly help feed our biological heart. It's the immaterial heart that the Bible tells us is very important and our physical heart is there as a representation of it. When a baby is born into this world, his first act is to breathe in, inhale, or inspire. When that same baby grows and gets old, the last act he performs will be to breathe out or to expire, which is why someone is said to have expired when they die.

Jesus cried out with a loud voice and released His spirit (Matt 27:50). The crying out was His expiring or breathing out. The "spire" in the words "inspire" and "expire," indicate spirit.[4] We can see how God is showing us something of how our spirit enters, and subsequently leaves, our bodies by using the physical air as a parallel. Plato's "shadow and reality" examples continue everywhere we look—each night we lay our bodies down in the static stupor we call sleep. Each morning we wake and begin to move, performing our daily tasks until we arrive at the end of the day and fall into slumber once again. The cycle continues, until one day we will fall into the sleep of death, from which we will awake in the resurrection. The scenario we act out each 24 hours of our lives is a mere shadow of the reality of death and resurrection.

We begin to see that spiritual realities are represented by physical events in space-time. William Blake referred to it as "fearful symmetry" in his poem "*The Tyger*."[5] Symmetry impregnates our daily lives. Some are too blind to see or too

4. *Concise Oxford Dictionary*, 1341.
5. Blake, *Songs of innocence and experience*, "The Tyger."

deaf to hear. That's why Jesus appealed to those with ears to hear when he said, "Look at the birds of the air," "Consider the lilies of the field" (Matt 6:26, 28). He spoke of the mustard seed, corn, swine, and dogs. He even used the slyness of the fox in reference to Herod. He showed us that what a man sows he also reaps. These are lessons written into the fabric of the universe; Jesus reminded us to look around and learn. Locked into the universe are shadows of spiritual reality.

Behind all our actions is a weight that far outweighs the action itself. To some it is a weight of glory—the Apostle Paul said he did not consider suffering in the present life worthy of comparison with the glory that shall be revealed. To others it is a weight sinking them to the lowest hell. Every action somehow binds or loosens something in the place of spiritual reality—what we bind on earth will be bound in heaven (Matt 18:18). "For our light and momentary troubles are achieving for us an eternal glory that far outweighs them all. So we fix our eyes not on what is seen, but on what is unseen. For what is seen is temporary, but what is unseen is eternal" (2 Cor 4:17–18). We are intrinsically linked to a spiritual dimension. To some it is the kingdom of light, being seated with Christ in heavenly realms (Eph 2:6). To others it is the domain of darkness whereby the tongue is set on fire by hell itself (Jas 3:6).

It is said that the writer Charles Williams had a "firm conviction that the spiritual world is not simply a reality parallel with that of the material one, but is rather its source and its abiding infrastructure."[6] I think this was something Charles tried to reveal in his books of fiction.

I could write out a cheque to the value of $1,000 but if the money is not in the bank, the cheque is worthless. The cheque is an indicator of something else. In the same way, the physical world is an indicator of something else. For example,

---

6. Williams, *War in Heaven*, back cover.

have you ever walked into a room full of strangers feeling slightly ill at ease and self-conscious? Yet if one of those strangers walks over to you, smiles, and shakes your hand, you suddenly feel less tense and are able to relax and fit in with the proceedings. What took place were a few mechanical actions in the physical world—a smile and a handshake. Small though these movements are, they reveal something important at an unseen level. Just as the cheque reveals what is in my account to the person named on the cheque, the smile and handshake also reveal what was hidden up to that point, namely friendliness towards you. Our actions are indicators of true reality; we are all connected to that unseen spiritual dimension in the same way as we all breathe the same air.

Of course the person who came up to us and shook our hand may have an ulterior motive, he may actually appear friendly because he wants to curry favor. Maybe he wants to sell us something, steal from us, or perhaps we are his new manager at work. There could be a host of reasons why he is trying to ingratiate himself into our good books. The cheque being of no value if the money is not in the bank is exactly the same as the actions of the person who is only appearing to be friendly. Such a person has an empty spiritual bank account. When you come to draw on his friendship, when you are in need, you will find that he is, as the proverb tells us, a cloud without rain (Prov 25:14).

Jesus told us to lay up treasures for ourselves in heaven (Matt 6:20). The modern mind thinks of heaven as something yet to come, but I don't think Jesus taught in this light. The sky-heaven from which He drew His parallel was with the people as He spoke, the true heaven is right here with us too. It may be a different dimension and we may not be able to see it, but the child of God is attached to it as some people are intrinsically linked to hell, the immoral woman's house of Proverbs 7 descended directly to Sheol, the place of the dead. Some people breathe the dank spiritual air of the devil's domain and others breathe the clean fresh air of God's kingdom. So, the person with a good heart who shakes our hand has treasures in heaven from which to draw. The man-pleaser that shakes our hand does not. Whether we can tell if someone's heart is good or bad from a handshake is not ours to judge; it is for God to decide. The handshake is an indicator, as each good or bad action accounts for an increase in our credit status in heaven or our debit in hell.

Ebenezer Scrooge asked his ghostly visitor Jacob Marley, "What is that chain you are wearing?" Marley answered, "I made this chain in life, link by link and yard by yard." Then he struck fear into Scrooge's cold heart by explaining that Scrooge had one too, just as heavy and just as thick, but Scrooge had had seven more years to forge his so it was much longer. It wasn't too hard for people to recognize whether Scrooge had a good or bad heart—by their fruit you shall know them (Matt 12:33). We don't have to wait long for the bad heart to show itself; our sins always find us out (Num 32:23).

We can see how small physical actions reveal something spiritual: The Christmas song "*Jingle Bells*" contains the lyrics, "Bells on Bob-tail ring, making spirits bright . . ." Can a few tiny bits of metal banging together make our spirits bright? Yes they can, especially when we are children. Tiny actions can have big results. Our spirits can be made bright by the vibrating of strings over a sound hole, by someone expelling air through their vocal chords, also by a handshake, a smile, and a thousand other things. When someone has been bereaved, how important it is to let them know that our heart towards them is good. A small gesture, such as sending a card or phoning them to say how sorry we are to hear of their loss, can mean so much. Each man is an island, so we need to reach out to each other through the medium of the physical world in which we all surface.

Fearing an adverse reaction, Christians sometimes temper their praise of God whilst in the company of the general public. But David says that he would "give thanks unto thee, O Lord, among the heathen and sing praises unto thy name" (Ps 18:49 KJV). If tinkling bells on a bobsleigh stir our hearts, how much more will they be moved when we hear the anthems that proclaim the worth of the living God? Our hearts will be stirred when we see or hear the sincere worship of God. The part of our being that has its roots in the immaterial unseen dimension of spirit cannot help but be moved. Christ said, "When I am lifted up I will draw all men to me" (John 12:32).

Men may resist the drawing with all their might, making a big show of their disapproval by covering up any feelings of being drawn. But still the drawing will occur: each man will feel the tug because God "has put eternity within the heart of man" (Eccl 3:11). An ordinary joyful act, such as giving thanks before a meal, can cause unendurable embarrassment for some at the table. I was once asked to give thanks at a Christmas meal where a number of people were present at the table. But one man could not endure what was for him, the ridiculous practice of religious zealots, so he announced that he was starting his dinner now. While the rest of us bowed our heads and gave thanks, we were accompanied by the sound of his chewing and clattering. Something within him was stirred to such an extent that he was prepared to allow those of us present to think him impolite and selfish, rather than acquiesce to giving thanks to the Lord. If he did not believe, he could have chosen to show respect for those of us who did. If not respect, couldn't he have humored us? In private I found out that he did have a belief in God, but it seemed he couldn't cope with the act of reverence towards Him. (Sounds to me like another deist.)

My father once visited a man who was quite ill. Though there were several people in the room when he arrived, he thought he ought to offer to pray for the sick man. The man willingly accepted the offer. Later I heard that the man's sister who was in the bedroom at the time of the prayer had said, "I nearly died of embarrassment when that man began to pray. I hope he doesn't do anything like that again."

But pray we must. If Christians don't give reverence, worship, and praise, then the rocks will cry out. Which they have, as a scant look across most European landscapes reveals: the gothic architecture of church spires and steeples made from rock speak volumes to those willing to listen. God has made it so He confronts men at every turn. As a postscript to this story, the sister of the ill man became sick herself some months later. My mother, knowing the lady's reaction to my father's prayer, still felt compelled to pay her a visit and ask if she would like prayer. Surprisingly, the lady willingly accepted my mother's offer of prayer and wanted to know more about God. Praising God will always cause a reaction: sometimes good, sometimes bad. God inhabits the praises of His people (Ps 22:3) and those who don't know the Lord may not be prepared for His presence being thrust upon them. In the book of Revelation, men call to the rocks to hide them from the face of Him who sits on the throne. Love burns like a hot iron when it is resisted. The fire that keeps a house warm can also burn that house to the ground if it's not attended to. God is love, and for those who love His appearing, He is precious. But, for those who are hardened inside, God's love can shatter their brittle heart. If we bury our heart in the ground, just like the man did with his talent (Matt 25:18), it will grow hard, useless, and well past its use-by date. The light will be too strong for its moldy exterior.

Acts of praise done in public will make waves. Whether we say, "God bless" at the end of the evening to people we've just met or sing with a worship group in a shopping mall, our praise will reach down into the hearts of men and women and solicit a response. Some ice-cold hearts will begin to melt while others crack from the sudden heat. Be prepared for those that crack open, because their contents will spill out. It was Jesus who said that it is what comes out of the heart that defiles a man: "For out of the heart proceed evil thoughts, murders, adulteries, sexual immorality, theft, false testimony and slander" (Matt 15:19). For some people, praising God in public is a bit like the nurse who rips the sticking plaster, hairs and all, off an injured man to reveal an open wound. Though a man needs to have his wound attended to, he's not going to relish the sight of seeing the robust nurse walking up his path. Christians are like the nurse, our praise will lay bare men's hearts, and as we know, some patients react badly when having their wounds dressed. "If people persecute you, rejoice, for great is your reward in heaven" (Matt 5:11–12).

Failing to see the spiritual infrastructure that underpins the material world means we're looking only at temporary things, the shadows. But, if we look at the realities themselves, even though they're unseen, it sets us apart from the world. He who is unseen made what is seen. This world is not our home; the Christian's real home is in heaven. But, do we live like it is? Nothing in this world can survive, just like a department store's closing down sale, "everything must go." Flesh and blood cannot inherit the kingdom of God; heaven and earth will pass away (1 John 2:17; Matt 24:35).

How does it look from God's point of view? Each new generation comes along with more than its share of strong, young people all using their strength, intellect, and good looks to jockey for position as if this world is their home and they'll be living here for ever. The Scriptures appeal to us: do not love the world for the world and its desires will pass away (1 John 2:17), whoever puts his trust in riches will fall (Prov 11:28), and what does it profit a man if he gains the whole world and loses his own soul (Matt 16:26)? As for man, he is like the grass of the field that springs up boldly in the morning but withers away under the heat of the mid-day sun. Strength, then, comes not from what we see, but what we don't see, strength for service and power to praise in the face of adversity.

5

Corporate Praise

My wife, Lorraine, and I visited a little girl on her birthday; there were several adults present. Before we left, we asked the girl if anyone had sung "*Happy Birthday*" to her yet. Thinking she would say, "yes" because it was late in the day, she surprised us by saying, "no." So Lorraine and I spontaneously burst into a lively version of "*Happy Birthday.*" We were about halfway through when I noticed the singing seemed remarkably thin for so many people—naturally we thought everyone would join in. We were wrong. As I looked around, I saw other adults sheepishly standing with their heads half bowed, ineptly hiding embarrassed grins. What, I wondered, hems people in so much that they can't sing "*Happy Birthday*" to a little girl on her birthday?

Singing is one of the tools a Christian uses. It is true that occasionally people sing together in bars, but it's usually later in the evening when Dutch courage has played its part. Even the Bible mentions drunkards who sing (Ps 69:12). Football supporters, too, have short bursts of what could be construed as singing—lager can help here, too. I've also heard of singers who summon up the strength to perform by taking drugs. The Christian needs no artificial help to sing; we sing because we want to. What arid dry territory the soul is in that cannot sing? A short while before Jesus was arrested He sang with

His disciples, much the same as an army would march into battle with a song.

The Church has a long history of music; when we meet, we sing. Though I suppose not all individuals who attend a service will necessarily feel like singing. Maybe sadness, grief, or depression has entered their lives. Though the majority would feel like singing, a few would not. If we are candid, there are times when many of us do not feel like singing the announced hymn and a groan rumbles from deep within us. However, not wishing to seem out of sorts, we begin to go through the motions and mumble the hymn. We may wonder if we're being hypocritical singing a hymn when we don't feel like it. Yet, as we heave our tired frame into an upright position, the mold is being cast. As we listen to the singing of the congregation, the die comes together. As we contemplate the words of the hymn, the ladle begins to pour and the molten liquid hardens as we find ourselves singing praises to the Lord from our hearts. The die breaks open to reveal a person worshipping God in spirit and in truth. Previously, what had been the shell of a human being going through the motions becomes a vital person filled with God's Spirit offering true praise. At the beginning of a church service we may well be the imitation of a person praising God, as all molds are only the inverted shapes of an object and not the object itself. If we apply ourselves even though we don't feel like it, any act of praise—praying, singing a hymn, kneeling, raising our hands, waving flags, or dancing—or participation in the corporate act of worship can lead us into a genuine expression of praise that delights God's heart with its sincerity. The important thing is that we make the attempt. Making the attempt is worship itself because it reveals that our heart is willing despite all obstacles in our way.

I sometimes teach people to play the guitar. The student who has made an attempt to play a piece but fails to execute the music correctly may be disheartened, but I am not. I know the very attempt itself is profitable. Unless attempts are made, the student will never play any piece of music; the failed attempts eventually lead to a successfully executed piece of music that is a pleasure to listen to.

Now it could be that, at certain times, a complete church service fails to reach us, even though we may have made the attempt to join in the acts of worship. First, I think it is uncharitable to blame the leader of the service if we are left unmoved by the singing, prayers, and preaching. I have heard ministers blamed for not being able to feed the flock. If that were true, God is able to remove the shepherd from his post. I tend to think the onus is upon us to apply ourselves to the food being offered.

Secondly, a church meeting is like a mold being cast, or perhaps a map designed to get us where we need to go. Jesus said, "Do this in remembrance of me" (Luke 22:19), on which we base the communion service. Baptism is another kind of service. Good men throughout the ages have also instituted rites, rituals, and acts of reverence. When these are truly followed, as a traveller follows a map, we will also arrive at the place where we offer heartfelt thanks and praise. Some churches are lively and have the latest worship music to sing with a fine band leading the worship. Other churches follow an orthodox route, preferring the order of service to be written down. Whatever type of church we attend, we have to apply ourselves to what is taking place and we have to do it with an open heart. Those who truly worship, as Jesus said, worship in spirit and in truth (John 4:23–24).

Some maps cover large areas, taking the traveller days, weeks, or even months to get to his journey's end. Weeks, too, may go by of cold-hearted hymn singing whereby the heavens seem like brass, and our acts of corporate praise make us feel like hypocrites. How important it is at this stage to keep on going and holding faithful to the map. We may be a slow traveller, but faithfulness delights God's heart; He will once again quench our thirsty soul. "You will seek me and find me when you search for me with all your heart" (Jer 29:13). We want people close to us who really love us. God does too; He's not into lack-lustre relationships.

I notice that the Jehovah's Witnesses tell us that Jesus was fond of the sons of men.[1] Somehow, I find it hard to equate the word "fond" with Jesus. I am fond of an ice cream now and again, but I'm not really bothered if I don't get one. Jesus was passionate, flinging over tables, crying out in a loud voice, weeping, and telling us to love with all our hearts. The word "fond" doesn't seem to attach itself very well to Jesus. God doesn't want us to be fond of Him, He wants us to love Him with all of our heart, soul, and strength because that's the way He loves us. As a deer pants for the streams of water, so our soul pants for God; He is the water of life we need. Jesus stood and said in a loud voice, "If any man is thirsty, let him come to me and drink" (John 7:37).

Journeys through the desert come to us all; Jesus was in the wilderness for forty days, Moses for forty years. The way across the desert is to stay true to the map. To sing a worship song with enthusiasm at times of dryness may seem a small and futile gesture, but showing ourselves faithful in small things is a key to being successful in the big things. If we show ourselves faithful to Him in small things, He will show Himself faithful to us in large things. "Those who honor me I will honor" (1 Sam 2:30). The Lord watches over our progress in times of sorrow, barrenness, and despair, and in some way, they stand us in good stead for times ahead. One reason being, we will be able to help others navigate their way through the wilderness. The Apostle Paul said, "Praise be to the God of all comfort, who comforts us in our troubles, so

---

1. The Watchtower, "*Angels—How They Affect Us*," paragraph 3.

that we can comfort those in trouble with the comfort we ourselves have received from God" (2 Cor 1:4).

But, perhaps the main reason we go through hard times is that God breathed the breath of life into us; we have a living soul. Some people do not take care of their souls, some souls fall into a state of disrepair, and some men lose their souls. We will all have to give an account of what we have done with our soul. It is possible to gain the whole world but lose your own soul. The point I am making is that walking through a spiritual desert is exercise for the soul; it is building up our inner man much like training to run a marathon is exercise for the body. Having a strong, healthy soul gives us integrity and inner strength, just like the tree planted by a river in Psalm 1 gives up its fruit in the proper season.

Integrity ensures that we tell the truth even though the truth may get us into trouble, it helps us keep a promise we have made even though it hurts, and it helps us keep our mouth shut when speaking would betray something we have been told in confidence. Having a strong soul makes us more like Jesus, and God wants all His children to be like His only begotten Son. Having a weak, unhealthy soul means we'll give in to temptation easily, show no restraint once we get talking, and give up when the going gets tough.

God gave us a body; it's up to us to take care of it and build it up. He also gave us our soul, which we need to feed and build up. If we fail to exercise our soul, it will weaken and suffer atrophy. We could even eventually lose it, becoming like brute beasts—we've all seen people who act like animals. Animals are material entities; humans are material and yet have something that is immaterial at the heart of our being. God breathed it into us or, we could say, *spirited* it into us. Animals don't have that: "Horses are flesh and not spirit" (Isa 31:3). Asaph said that when his heart was grieved and his spirit embittered, he was like a brute beast before God (Ps 73:22). What a privilege we have that

God's breath is central to our being; what folly that we give it up so cheaply. We need to grow into the image of Christ more and more, not into the image of beasts.

When someone has a broken leg, it is set, and during this period the muscle begins to waste. Once the plaster is taken off, the physical therapist gets to work building it up by giving the patient load-bearing exercises to perform. God is giving us load-bearing exercises to perform when we go through hard times; they will build us up. God's plans are to build us up and not break us down. "I pray that out of His glorious riches He may strengthen you with power through His Spirit in your inner being" (Eph 3:16).

Some people excuse themselves from regularly going to church by saying that God is with them on the golf course just as much as He is with them in church. It is true that God is with us on the golf course, but in a special way, Christ is present where two or three are gathered together in His name. The biblical injunction is, "Don't stop meeting together" (Heb 10:25).

Jesus said, "The wind blows where it pleases . . . so it is with everyone born of the Spirit" (John 3:8). There needs to be more than one person present for the wind of the Spirit to blow. If we are by ourselves, the wind of the Spirit may be in us and upon us and may stir our souls. But, in order for the Spirit to blow, there needs to be some space involved. Movement is indicated by the word "blow." The wind of the Spirit blows from one person to another.

First Corinthians 14:26 tells us, "When you assemble, each one has a psalm, has a teaching, has a revelation, has a tongue, has an interpretation." These offerings are brought by means of the Spirit blowing through us to others. We may be feeling low on our arrival at church, but the Holy Spirit has something to say to us, and He will say it by using other people to minister to us. They may not be aware that they are even ministering to us, because this is a work of the

Spirit and not of our mind. We may also be taken by surprise by the vessel the Holy Spirit chooses to blow through; it may be the most unlikely person there.

The pastor of my church once asked the children to go out into the congregation and pray for the people. My first reaction was, "Oh, that's sweet," but then something or someone, told me not to patronize the children but to enter into what the pastor had asked them to do. A youngster came and placed her hands on my head and prayed to God on my behalf. I was truly blessed. The innocence of her prayer took me by surprise, and I was quite broken. It turned out to be a very special service that made an impression on me, and in which I learned an important lesson. We don't see the wind, but we feel its effects. The wind of the Spirit was blowing through the children that Sunday morning. Next Sunday it could be someone else.

Secondly, we don't meet together as people meet together for a good time "down at the old Bull and Bush," neither do we meet to pass a pleasant ninety minutes being taken out of ourselves watching a few people do a "turn" on stage. Something very important happens when Christians meet together to praise God.

"Would a man rob God," asked God of the Israelites? "Yet you have robbed me," came the Lord's response (Mal 3:8). If we rob our landlord by not paying the rent when it is due, we may face eviction. Similarly, our supply of gas will be cut off if the gas bill is due and we fail to pay it. There are consequences if we do not pay what we owe when it is due. The earth and everything in it is the Lord's, yet the world does not give Him what is due. We are asked to "Ascribe to the LORD the glory due to His name" (Ps 29:2). We live on His earth and eat His food; the cattle on a thousand hills belong to Him. Yet, some men fail to thank or praise Him. We praise our wife, children, and our dog, yet we neglect to give our Creator the glory due to His name. We glorify footballers, film stars, and rock singers. We worship our homes, cars, and careers, but fail to give God what is due to Him. Footballers let us down, our careers may be the cause of divorce, our cars may crash, our homes slowly fall to bits, but God never lets us down; He is always working at ways to bless us with goodness.

I saw a TV documentary a couple of days ago in which a murderer had been brought to justice by a series of coincidences. The perpetrator had killed a man who was a guest on his boat; he weighted the dead man's body and threw it into the sea. There were no witnesses as they had been the only two people on the boat and the boat was in a remote part of the sea. Seven days later a fishing trawler happened to fish in this part of the sea that is rarely fished. The dead man's body happened to catch in their net and the fishermen immediately reported it to the police. In another unrelated matter, the police had found a discrepancy with the murderer's personal details. Upon questioning him, they found he had contact with the murdered man. Cutting a long story short, some fine police work soon uncovered the whole chain of events. The man is now serving a life prison sentence. I couldn't help but see God's handiwork involved in this story. God is very interested in justice; after all, it was He who gave us the Ten Commandments. God is at work in the world all the time, but some people fail to see it. Some people may see the story in the documentary as a chain of amazing coincidences. Not me. I praise God that He is interested in justice, and will help us in our pursuit of justice when we cannot help ourselves.

Christians meet together to help redress the balance—to give God our Father something of what is due to Him. God was about to obliterate Sodom and Gomorrah from the face of the earth when Abraham asked the question: If ten righteous people could be found in the wicked city would God spare it (Gen 18:32)? The Lord agreed and said

He wouldn't destroy the city if ten righteous people could be found. But ten righteous people could not be found. Lot and his two daughters were the only righteous people saved as they escaped on foot.

We have a charge from God not to appear before Him empty-handed (Exod 23:15). Some people fail to offer God what is due to Him. Maybe it is here that we begin to see a little of what Christ meant when He called His followers "the salt of the earth." Salt is a preservative. You don't need a lot of salt to make a difference in a meal; ten righteous people would have been enough to preserve Sodom and Gomorrah. (Lot's wife should have been salt but she looked back and ended up becoming salt along with the plains of Sodom and Gomorrah. This area is now said to be in the Dead Sea, which is one of the saltiest seas in the world, and the lowest place on earth—in more ways than one.)

If I owe money on rent that is overdue and someone offers to pay it for me, my tenancy will stay intact a little longer. Maybe Christians are going some way towards paying the rent for others. When God sees that every thought and imagination of man is wholly evil, something has to be done; it was in Noah's day and it will be in ours. "For it is because of these things that the wrath of God will come upon the sons of disobedience" (Col 3:6; Eph 5:6). Lot's family was taken out of Sodom just prior to its destruction. It looks to me like there is a similarity between their age and ours. Whatever our eschatological thoughts and beliefs, God calling in the debt at some point is worth thinking about.

The world's lack of praise for God may be the catalyst that leads us into "Jacob's Trouble" (Jer 30:7). Desperate situations demand desperate measures and God will allow humankind to follow its own course, letting them see how bad evil is, that people might turn to Him and be rescued. "Jacob's Trouble" or Armageddon or the Great Tribulation—whatever people want to call it—will be a severe mercy, not an easy ride. The debt of praise may cripple this present age that even now groans under its weight. The deficit can become greater than any known economic debt. It can send this world into a spiritual bankruptcy from which it will not recover until it has paid the very last penny, and all bend their knees to acknowledge that Jesus Christ is Lord. Ten righteous people could not be found in Sodom, and what happened there serves as an example to posterity.

So, our church meetings—small though they may be—accomplish something very important. Ordinary people, giving glory to God through their varied forms of worship, go some way toward staving off God calling in the global debt of ingratitude, presumption, and rebellion. A church service cannot, of course, make a down payment on each individual's eternal salvation, as if it is somehow possible to purchase a ticket for heaven. Christ alone paid the debt with His blood. This temporary sphere on which we sojourn will one day be destroyed with fervent heat; it is the presence of those made righteous through Christ that helps defer that dreadful hour.

It is worth mentioning that all God has to do for calamity to come upon us is to leave us alone. Sin is its own punishment. Our own devices will ensure that destruction comes. A parent, when pushed to the limit, will sometimes say to their child, "Okay then, have it your way," knowing that trouble will ensue. The parent's heart is still good towards the child, but relinquishes charge over the child for a period of time. God's Spirit will not always strive with men. "If my people, who are called by my name, will humble themselves and pray and seek my face and turn from their wicked ways, then I will hear from heaven and will forgive their sin and will heal their land" (2 Chr 7:14). If we do not do those things, He will not heal our land.

Christ could have stayed in the comfort of the upper room. Instead, He set His face as a flint and went out into the night, knowing what awaited Him. We have every reason to get up off the sofa, turn off the TV, put on our coat, and make our way to church. When we get there, we can inject some life into those songs, say "amen" to that prayer with sincerity, and apply ourselves to righteousness. The Apostle Paul said, "I beat my body and make it a slave" (1 Cor 9:27). The Lord sees all our efforts—leaving the warm house, making our tired legs carry us to church—it is all accepted as part of our praise and worship, just as much as singing one of Charles Wesley's hymns.

There are many temptations that come our way to hinder us from taking part in corporate praise. If we can identify them—become aware of the devil's devices—we are better able to resist them. We do not wrestle against flesh and blood, but against spiritual wickedness in high places. Unseen eyes see our worship. The early church was well aware of the presence of spiritual beings. A woman ought to be covered because of the angels, said St. Paul to the Corinthians (1 Cor 11:10), probably referring to the angels who lost their position for looking at the daughters of men and lying with them to produce offspring. They also knew that some people entertained angels unawares. They thought it could be Peter's angel knocking at the door. When the early Christians proclaimed that God is good and Jesus is Lord, they knew it wasn't only God and humans who heard.

God spoke to Satan saying, "Have you considered my servant Job?" Satan replied, "Does Job fear God for nothing? Strike everything he has and he will curse you to your face" Job 1:8–11). It is as if God is even saying something to spiritual beings through our worship. Job stayed true to God, which has earned him an eternal decoration—many have heard the phrase "the patience of Job." The principalities saw a faithful man who loved God when they watched Job. Satan brought disaster, grief, illness, friends, and his own wife to undermine his faith in God. But in all of this,

Job did nothing wrong, saying, "The Lord gave and the Lord has taken away; may the name of the Lord be praised" (Job 1:21). Even the angels, says Peter, long to look into these things. It seems, then, that our songs of praise, prayers, and good confessions that Jesus is Lord, reach much further than the congregation.

6

Misplaced Praise

As you are reading this book, heaven's inhabitants are praising God. It would be good if the inhabitants of earth were, too. But on the whole, modern man is stealing God's glory and failing to give God what is due. God is robbed in education, politics, and the media. How many school textbooks give God credit for creation? How many politicians give thanks when the land enjoys times of peace and prosperity? How many newspapers, radio, and TV stations present a caricatured God of their own making? His divine attributes are belittled, His power questioned, and praise that ought to have been directed towards God is redirected towards abstract gods like "Mother Nature" or "Natural Selection." God looked at all He had made and certified it as good. We accept that creation is good but deny that God created it. "Random Chance" just so happened to accidentally make a good universe. It might just as easily have made a bad one, but it didn't, it made a brilliant one—a universe too incredibly exquisite for words.

I find that a deep desire stirs within me to praise the wonders my eyes see and ears hear, but who shall I praise, the "Laws of Physics?" How can I praise a label? Deep within our hearts is the desire to praise; our enjoyment is somehow incomplete until we have praised the object that captured our attention.

When I read about the human gene, I am filled with wonder. For example, there are 3.1 billion letters in the DNA code in every cell of the 100 trillion cells in the human body.[1] If all of the DNA in the human body were put end to end, it would reach to the sun and back more than 600 times.[2] The gene turns hundreds of revolutions per second in order to regroup within the twenty minutes it takes a cell to divide. Deoxyribonucleic acid (DNA) has just four letters (or chemicals), yet it manages to encode and transmit all the information necessary to create a living creature, from the lowliest bacteria to the mighty blue whale to us. In 1953, James Watson and Francis Crick finally came up with a model of DNA structure: the famous "double helix." Two strands of DNA run parallel to each other. DNA replicates itself by the double helix unzipping and a new strand forms on each half of the unzipped helix and is a perfect copy 999,999,999 times out of a billion. Of course, all of this happens much more quickly than a description makes it sound. In the last second, your body created about 500 trillion faultless copies of hemoglobin, a protein containing more than 570 amino acids.[3] Each cell contains a family of more than thirty enzymes (the enzymes are called DNA polymerase) to insure the accurate replication of DNA, and DNA polymerase and other enzymes "proofread" the new DNA strand. DNA replication is extraordinarily accurate. If a newly added nucleotide (nucleotides are the structural units of DNA) is not complementary to the one on the template strand, these enzymes remove the nucleotide and replace it with the correct one. With this system, a cell's DNA is copied with less than one mistake

---

1. BBC News, http://news.bbc.co.uk/1/hi/sci/tech/115172.stm, lines 9–11.

2. Briggs, BBC News, http://news.bbc.co.uk/1/hi/sci/tech/1426702.stm, lines 11–17.

3. Willett, http://www.edwardwillett.com/Columns/dna.htm.

in a billion nucleotides. This is equal to a person copying 100 large (1000 page) dictionaries word for word, symbol for symbol, with only one error for the whole process![4]

I'm filled with awe and inspired to praise as David did saying, "You created my inmost being; you knitted me together in my mother's womb. I praise you because I am fearfully and wonderful made; your works are wonderful, I know that full well" (Ps 139:13–14).

How those who doubt cope when hearing the wonderful facts of creation, I'm not sure. It can't be easy: "I'm really glad 'Random Chance' just happened to give us eyes, or we might bump into things." The world misplaces the praise that ought to go to God. It is almost as if it's a strategic plan by some enemy. The praise is there to give and plain to see but somehow people's eyes are darkened and they miss it.

God's glory is stolen in the animal kingdom. People often sit transfixed to the TV watching nature programs; it's a testimony to God's amazing creativity that there are so many nature programs to watch. These shows make excellent television and people want to see them. How on earth do salmon find their way back to their freshwater breeding grounds? Naturalists on the programs tell us plainly that salmon find their way back through instinct. But if we stop to give it some thought, instinct is a name for, we know not what. We may wonder about the migratory ability of fish and birds, but we don't get closer to finding out how they do it by saying "they do it through instinct." It's the classic "reductio ad absurdum," Latin for "proof by contradiction":

"What is instinct?"
"It's what animals do."
"I see, and why do they do it the way they do?"
"Well, they do it because of instinct."

4. Contexo.info, http://www.contexo.info/DNA_Basics/DNA%20Replication.htm.

Seeing something we don't understand and giving it a name does not help us understand it any better. When naturalists present a one-hour TV program explaining how homing pigeons find their way home through instinct, they might as well be up front at the beginning of the show and say, "Sorry, we don't know how they do it." It is a mystery to them; Christians agree it is a mystery. God works in mysterious ways His wonders to perform. Some people who listen to the TV shows and hear that animals perform their marvelous feats of navigation by instinct may go away thinking, "I always wondered how migratory birds know when to fly south and now I know, it's through instinct, well how about that!" Credit is given to the metaphysical god of instinct and no acknowledgement given to the Creator. No one is quite sure, but the people on TV seem to know, so the general consensus is that it must be true—they wouldn't put things on TV that weren't true would they? It is one more feature in the catalogue of misplaced praise.

My son and I were checking out a few websites about the moon. Someone emailed a question to one site that said, "Why is the moon exactly the same apparent size from earth as the sun? Surely this cannot be just coincidence; the odds against such a perfect match are enormous." The astronomical site they had written to said: "Believe it or not, it actually is just a coincidence,"[5]

I wondered how many coincidences do people want before they'll use the word "design?" Other sites use words like "uncanny," "extraordinary," and "amazing" to describe the total eclipse of the sun, which is caused by the moon's size and distance lining up perfectly with the sun. I can't help but think God is showing us His perfect timing. I have

---

5. Naeye, Astronomy.com, http://www.astronomy.com/asy/default.aspx?c=a&id=2196, line 1.

often seen it in my own life; the moon and planets show it in another way.

> The heavens declare the glory of God; the skies proclaim the work of His hands. Day after day they pour forth speech; night after night they display knowledge. There is no speech or language where their voice is not heard. Their voice goes out into all the earth, their words to the ends of the world. (Ps 19:1–4)

I'm so glad that David recognized God's handiwork in the skies; now it is written for all the earth in every generation to read just in case they, like some astronomers, refuse to see God's hand in it. I find myself to be jealous for God's glory; I'm concerned that He isn't praised, which is one of the reasons I'm writing this book. Scripture informs us well before the astronomers do, yet they think they are telling us something we don't know. It's no wonder God laughs at them (Ps 2). In the 1920s, Edwin Hubble and Milton Humason discovered that the universe is not static, but is expanding. As the universe expands, it is being stretched out, rather like a balloon being blown up; Einstein's theory of relativity is being proved correct. Isaiah 45:12 and other Bible verses tell us, "My own hands, have stretched out the heavens." The Bible mentions the word "stretched," which is the very word cosmologists use to explain what is happening to space-time.

We show our appreciation to our friends who give us birthday cards, shouldn't we thank Him who allowed us to be born? We give our compliments to the chef for serving fine food, isn't something within us grateful to Him who causes food to grow? People would rather read their horoscopes than praise Him who put the stars in their place. They have no faith that He who calls the stars by name also has a place for them in the universe. They thank their lucky stars rather than thanking God for His divine providence. Ronnie Barker, the great British comedian, said two words sum up his very productive career: "What luck." I like Ronnie a lot but I wonder why the god of luck received praise but the living God received none. God called the stars into place and He also called us. He steers the celestial bodies on their courses; He also has a route marked out for us if we will follow.

Everywhere we find ourselves, God has a place for us. Before we were born He had a little section of time and space marked out just for us. We fit into the mosaic of the universe exactly where He wants us. If we do wrong, He has a plan. Gravity will pull water down from the sky onto the earth and then down crevices, nooks, and crannies where it flows into streams, rivers, and eventually into the sea. If we watch the water carefully on its journey we may wonder what purpose there could be in such twisting, turning, splashing, and running. But, if the water remains water and doesn't turn into ice, it will arrive where it was meant to go. Ice remains cold and unforgiving; it goes nowhere. If we are humble and broken for every wrong turn we make, God has a contingency plan. Christ's blood cleanses us from all sin, and God works all things together for good for those who love Him.

When I find myself in a certain circumstance or location that I have a duty to be in but probably wouldn't have chosen for myself, I try to remember this is where I'm supposed to be in the grand scheme of things. I might as well make myself comfy, calm myself with the peace of Christ, and shine the light that God has given me to shine. Through His providence He has something to show me, someone to talk to, someone to listen to. God's favor is upon me to bless me in some way that I haven't yet experienced. Wherever I am, is where I'm supposed to be. I fit into the environment neatly; God has made a path through time and space for you and me. If we love and enjoy God and do to others as we would have them do to us, the path takes care of itself. His Word is a lamp unto my feet; all we have to do is walk in it. If we are hard like ice, we struggle to move, gaining a few meters by gouging great crevices out of our own local landscape with cursing, hatred, and hardness of heart. We become at odds with the environment, not fitting snugly, but careening out of control like a spinning top with its own centre of gravity, unable to conform to the general pull of God's love, and ricocheting off anything that happens to be in our way.

Praise for God's amazing providence is stolen when astrologists write horoscopes for newspapers and magazines telling us it's a good day for romance but not for making key decisions. Or, it's time to be creative, but not for talking to strangers. Star signs dictate what kind of a person someone will be until the day they die. God is made to look powerless and humankind's free will is hijacked. We are told to marry someone with a star sign congenial to our own, and go into business with someone whose star sign doesn't clash with ours.

The Canaanites were no different, they were so hemmed in it's a wonder they could walk down the street. In fact some days they couldn't. Their day could be ruined and fear struck into their hearts by the most simple of everyday occurrences which they saw as a bad omen: A morsel of food falling out of their mouth, dropping a staff, a child calling out behind them, a crow cawing to them, a deer crossing their path, a snake creeping on their right or a fox on their left—all these were considered a portent of evil design.[6]

The Israelites were told to completely disregard the enchantments, sorcery, and divination of the Canaanites. A man would inhale smoke from incenses that would send him into a drug-induced trance, the Canaanites would then

6. Ellicott, *Bible Commentary for English Readers*, 427.

listen to the babbling of the drug-taker whilst he was in his state of euphoria and regard his utterances as fortune telling which ought to be obeyed. God didn't want His people enslaved by stupid superstitions. There is no merit in superstition whatsoever; not a drop of sense or goodness can be wrung from it. Man was made in God's image with the ability to reason. Satan wants us to give up that image and be led about like beasts. I've heard people say, "Don't walk under a ladder, it's bad luck." We may think there is a drop of sense in that because the person at the top of the ladder might accidentally drop a can of paint on our head. It is equally true that you may get run over by a car as you step out into the road to avoid walking under the ladder. God expects us to use the brain He has given us and doesn't want us trapped by nonsense. The Israelites were told to rid the land of everyone who practiced such enslaving beliefs. The Lord walks with us through life providing (which is the root meaning of the word "providence") for each eventuality that happens to us. God's providence and our reason work like two figure skaters dancing together performing all kinds of amazing feats.

There is wonder in the world around us if we could only see it. As some people grow older they lose the wonder of life. In reality, life is magical, wondrous, and dazzling, but somehow the enemy manages to darken the eyes of some adults so they fail to see the awesome wonder of life and creation. Children don't seem to have a problem; every day to them is a day of excitement and interest. Sadly, the Hebrews themselves lost the wonder and fear of the living God and were evicted from the land they had been given. Part of the reason for the ejection was for taking on the superstitions of the surrounding nations. As if men have to inject some wonder and excitement into life because what God has created isn't good enough! It is exactly the same reason people take drugs; they're not content with life as God has made it. Christians take life as it comes to us, one day at a time.

We don't have to take chemicals to add something to our tired lives; the joy of the Lord is our strength. Jesus refused to take the wine mixed with gall that the soldiers offered Him, even though it was given as a soporific drug to blunt the edges of a condemned man's pain. Once He tasted it and realized what it was, He refused to drink it even though He had great thirst (Matt 27:34). Christ took life head on, whether in suffering or comfort. The Apostle Paul learned the same lesson: "I have learned to be content whatever the circumstances" (Phil 4:11).

The trouble with listening to Satan is that there is always a price to pay for his advice. Some solicitors may give a person free advice occasionally, but not this one. A local Canaanite sage could interpret an everyday ordinary event to mean anything he wanted. He could suddenly announce that the heathen god Molech wants the sacrifice of a child to appease his anger. Israel began to follow this detestable superstition, thinking the only way to placate the gods was to send their sons and daughters into the fire.[7] In response to this, the living God said the thought had never entered His head (Jer 7:31).

Of course there is a faint inkling of truth behind this ghastly business, which is what Satan may have used to beguile the people. It is true, sacrifice was used, and the sacrifice of a son, but not yours or mine or even Abraham's son (as God demonstrated) but the sacrifice of God's Son. It's also true that God was keen to illustrate this fact by symbols, types, and shadows in the Mosaic Law, but children were never used. It was the sacrifice of lambs and goats and other animals that God chose to show the truth of Christ's death. That is why Jesus is called the Lamb of the world. To use real, living, breathing children for sacrifice was craziness to God; the Israelites who sacrificed their children didn't

---

7. Unger, *Unger's Bible Dictionary*, 416.

know God at all. God states that no one will harm or destroy on His holy mountain (Isa 65:25). That is God's heart; He is a protector not a destroyer. Satan is a destroyer; his Greek name is *"Apollyon,"* which means just that: Destroyer.

Jesus came down hard upon the Pharisees and religious leaders because they didn't know God, yet they were teachers of the people. They were blind leaders of blind followers. In Christ we are free from living in fear of omens, signs, and portents. We live life with our free will and divine providence dancing together. We have to watch yielding to the human weakness of superstition. Even Bible readings can be said to be signs from God with meanings attached to them far removed from the context in which they were written. Innocuous events can be subjectively spiritualized beyond any natural function God intended them for. A local man who lived close to me wasn't content to grow strong in his own small church so he prayed that God would send him somewhere to do great things. Shortly after, he saw an advertisement for a Cadbury's Brazil Nut chocolate bar. He immediately presumed God was telling him to go to South America. It's a good thing he didn't see an advertisement for a Mars bar!

People have ended up in messes because of pseudo-spirituality, which at best is wishful thinking and at worst is pure superstition. The Lord has given us the objective Word of God in the full canon of Holy Scripture. If we prefer to trust our own subjective thoughts, we do it to our own detriment and sometimes, as the Israelites found out, to the detriment of our own families. The Bible isn't a Christian horoscope, but God's living Word meant to be read, studied, rightly divided, and acted upon. If we obey it in the context it is written, our lives will fall into place exactly how God wants them to be. Flicking open a page and reading the first verse you see isn't the way to read the Scriptures. I know a girl who did that more than once and read something like "God has rejected you." She took this to heart and it spoiled her walk with the Lord. It took her several years to get back to where she now walks before the Lord in a peaceful, joyful way. The people written about in the Bible learned important lessons and were blessed by them. We also will be blessed when we learn the same lessons. That is why the Bible is there, to help us learn lessons the easy way. Of course if we don't learn them the easy way, there is always another way.

I know God uses prophecy and the gifts of the Spirit to speak to us and when He does, it is for our edification; it brings light to us and sometimes tells us what will be. Not that we have to bring it about, but that God will bring it about in His own good time. Joseph had dreams about his family bowing down to him and eventually it took place, but not until much hardship had been endured (Gen 37, 39–50). Joseph couldn't cause it to happen by telling his brothers about his dreams. In fact, that had the opposite effect. They wanted to kill him not respect him. God doesn't seem to give us self-fulfilling prophesies, but sometimes wants us to know what He is going to do. I had a very vivid and unusual dream when I was sixteen; it lived with me for some time and it wasn't a pleasant dream at all. Sometime later, the very thing I had dreamt about happened to me. I was rushed to hospital as a result. God let me know that even though I was learning something the hard way, He was with me. It hadn't taken Him by surprise and to let me know, He gave me the dream months before the event took place. I learned a lot from that experience.

It is our job to know the Scriptures because they are able to make us wise to salvation through faith in Jesus Christ. They also help us to live a life that is pleasing to Him by equipping us to use the knowledge of His Word and the brain and reasoning powers He has given to us. Animals don't reason, that is something reserved for humans who were made in His image. God Himself reasons and expects us to do the same (Isa 1:18). The Apostle Paul used his brain to fulfill the commission given him. He planned his journeys to visit churches and cities. On one occasion he was kept from going into Asia and Bithynia, and then he had a vision of a man from Macedonia asking for help (Acts 16:9). James writes about what happened to Paul, "Be mature and complete not lacking anything. If any of you lacks wisdom, he should ask God, who gives generously to all" (Jas 1:4b–5).

Paul's plans had not worked out, but God allowed him to see a Macedonian who was appealing for help. Thus, Paul now had new information on which to base decisions. First Paul had to put his plans into action, and then God worked with him as a co-worker. We must do what we can, leaving God to do those things we can't. Most of Paul's plans did work out, but when he came to a standstill and wondered what to do next, God gave him another course of action from which to decide. However, in Acts 21:4 we find Paul urged by disciples in Tyre not to go to Jerusalem; they did this "through the Spirit." We don't get the feel of a command here, rather God's heart and the hearts of the disciples alerting Paul to trouble that awaited him at Jerusalem. Paul used his own mind and reasoning to put into plan the commission given him, which was to carry Jesus' name to Gentiles and kings and before the people of Israel. Therefore, he decides to go against the feelings of the Christians in Tyre and makes his way to Jerusalem.

Jesus said, "An adulterous and wicked generation look for a sign" (Matt 12:39). The Apostle Paul said, "Don't let anyone who delights in the worship of angels disqualify you for the prize. Such a person goes into great detail about what he has seen and his unspiritual mind puffs him up with idle notions" (Col 2:18). The world robs God of the praise due to Him for His gracious providence. We ought to make certain that it doesn't rob us of our freedom in Christ. Whom the Son sets free, is free indeed. It is in God we live, move, and have our being. Through the gifts of the Spirit He allows us to experience true prophecy, speak the languages of men and angels, and interpret what is said. He gives us faith that moves mountains, miracles that bring Him praise, and healing for the sick. We are given discernment of evil, knowledge the world knows nothing of, and finally, the wisdom to know when and where to use these gifts (1 Cor 12:8–10). Life in Christ is exciting. Christians don't need to read the stars; we trust in Him who made the stars.

Satan displays all kinds of counterfeit miracles, signs, and wonders that if it were possible, would deceive the very elect (2 Thess 2:9; Matt 24:24). Counterfeit means imitation, not the real thing. Counterfeit money is worthless, though some unsuspecting folk may be taken in by it. But, when they try to bank their money, they will find it is useless. It may look like money but was fraudulent and not legal tender. Counterfeit signs and wonders are not real miracles at all, but people are sent a strong delusion that they might believe a lie, and some people are taken in by counterfeit miracles. We have no need to be afraid of the dark, ghosts, ghouls, wraiths, witches, warlocks, or wizards. This is also true of portents, bad luck, or omens, and the like. We are in God's hands; Christ holds all things together.

Psalm 93:1 tells us, "The world is firmly established; it cannot be moved." God wants us to make good and right decisions, so He's made the universe we live in a stable environment in which to make those decisions. You can't ask a soccer player to score goals if the goal posts are constantly changing. God has made the laws of physics and they are good. He has given human beings free will in which to move around inside the laws of physics. The laws are the apparatus we use to make good or bad decisions. You can offer someone my chair if there's nowhere for them to sit, or you can put them into a position of not needing a chair by smashing the chair over their head. The chair remains a chair throughout either option. It doesn't remain hard while someone sits on it and then go soft when used to strike someone. It remains constant; that's the way God designed it. It is God's desire that we use our environment to help each other rather than hurt each other, but the option must be there in a world of creatures having free will. If the option for good and evil weren't there, we would be automata, androids, or robots and not made in God's image.

My ten-year-old son had a scary dream recently, in which weird things began to happen to the environment he found himself in. He called out to us. When I went into his bedroom he told me that he saw strange "light creatures" that had "hangy-down things" and they were able to distort things around him. I sat with him for a while until he was ready to sleep again. In the morning, he was still talking about the monsters he met in his dream. So, during breakfast, we looked at a few Scriptures that tell us we live in a solid and stable world. God has made it stable with laws that cannot be moved. The Bible tells us that "Faithfulness springs forth from the earth" (Ps 85:11), that the laws God has put in place stand firm (Ps 93:5), and "He set the earth on its foundations; it can never be moved" (Ps 104:5). I told my son that we never have to be scared of things that seem to be supernatural; we live in a natural world, with natural bodies in a universe that is governed by natural laws, laws that God has set in place. No one can bend them because God has said they are faithful. God has made them faithful, which tells us something about God. What He has made is faithful because He is faithful. He never changes. Jesus Christ: the same yesterday, today, and forever (Heb 13:8).

Even Christ seemed to work within the laws of nature when He performed wonders; He speeded up the natural process. God turns water into wine all the time, through rain, soil, vine roots, grapes, and men who tread the grapes. It takes a long time, but Jesus did it in an instant (John 2:1–12). The same as the feeding of the five thousand, God turns bread into more bread all the time, through the seeds of wheat that are planted each spring and by autumn there is a lot of wheat. It is the same with the fish, God is constantly multiplying the fish in the sea. In fact, all you need for the natural order that God has placed in the world to run its course is two fish. As long as they are male and female, the fish will do the rest. Jesus had exactly that: two fish. He sped up the process for the purpose of bringing glory to God and feeding the hungry people (Mark 6:38–44). What God does globally and over a period of time, Jesus did locally and instantly. Jesus said, "The Son can only do what He sees the Father doing" (John 5:19).

Other miracles have a similar theme. Storms pass after a few hours or days, yet Jesus instantly calmed the sea (Mark 4:39). Walking on the water is a natural thing to do, too. People sometimes walk on water to cross from Siberia to Alaska across the Bering Straits. Jesus didn't need to wait until water turned to ice, He has control of the elements; they serve Him. He was showing us something through the miracles. He was lowly of heart and didn't go round shouting the fact that He had created everything; He let His works speak for themselves. He spat into the ground and made mud, then put it on a blind man's eyes. When the man washed his face he had brand new eyes (John 9:6–7). That's just what God did at creation. He took a whole lot of mud and made a man.

Jesus did things the Father does. Perhaps that is why when he was tempted, Jesus wouldn't turn stone into bread—we don't see that done by the Father anywhere in the world. When Jesus healed, He did what God is doing all the time. When we get cut, we don't worry too much because we know the cut will heal if we keep it clean. Even if we break a bone, as long as it is held in place, it will heal. Jesus healed not over time, but in a moment.

The medical profession receives all the praise for curing our ills. Children are told, "The doctor will make you better." Doctors may tell us how to behave during an illness and may recommend medicine or a course of action to aid the healing process, but it is God who does the healing. The doctors do a magnificent job, but they don't heal us anymore than farmers cause crops to grow, or weather forecasters cause rain to fall, or nutritionists cause our bodies to digest the food we eat. People have gained knowledge about how the universe works, but that doesn't mean they make it work.

Jesus was showing us exactly who He was in the humble and lowly way He went about things. He rose from the dead—the first fruits of the resurrection—as we all will one day be raised from the dead, the righteous and the unrighteous (Rev 20:4b–5). The truth of the resurrection is written into the universe. The scenario is performed every twenty-four hours when we wake from a night's sleep. There is also autumn, which brings decay. Yet, each spring we see apparently dead things come to life. God is showing us something. We haven't seen our own resurrection yet, of course. People have to live and die before they can be resurrected and humankind haven't finished doing their living yet.

It is God who performs wonders and no one else. Satan had to have God's license to bring devastation on Job (Job 1:9–12), and then he only used natural—not supernatural—events such as raiders, lightning, a storm, and illness (Job 1:13–22, 2:1–7). The magicians of Egypt used enchantments to compete with Moses' miracles before Pharaoh (Exod 7:11, 22; 8:7, 18). Pharaoh was unwilling to let Moses and the Israelites go, so he looked to his wise men to convince him that Moses was doing nothing that they couldn't do. Pharaoh's magi performed adequately enough to satisfy Pharaoh, allowing him to harden his heart. The Hebraic word for enchantments is "*lehatim,*" which is covered by the modern day phrase "sleight of hand."[8] Unlike the magicians, Moses was no mere conjurer. By the third plague, which they found they could not mimic, even the magicians had to admit that Moses was working with the "finger of God" (Exod 8:18–19).

It is Christ who performs bona fide miracles. One of these is new birth, which sets us free from any foreboding of the paranormal. We need no fortune-teller. We have no fear of the future; we believe His Word. When our loved ones die we have no need of a necromancer to let us know they are okay in the nether world of the hereafter. We are told not to grieve like those who have no hope; we know that to be absent from the body is to be present with the Lord.

God wants us to stand before Him as a whole person made in His image, to be a Father and a friend to us. He talked with Adam in the cool of the day, referred to Abraham as His friend, and spoke with Moses face to face. He wants to talk to us too, saying, "Strengthen the feeble hands, steady the knees that give way; be strong and do not fear" (Isa 35:3; Heb 12:12). We praise Jesus Christ for the freedom He has given us to live and walk in His Spirit.

Some people are ashamed of Christ, only using His name as an expletive. They try to sweep Jesus under the carpet. I was talking in a school classroom some time ago when I noticed a history chart on the wall. On close inspection, the normal Latin AD for events after the birth of Christ had been exchanged for ACE. BC, for events before Christ's birth, had also been changed to BCE. I asked the teacher what the "E" stood for; did it have something to do with the European Economic Community? They seem to put E's on so many things. Or was it Internet related? She told me that ACE and BCE stand for After Common Era and Before Common Era, which have nothing to do with

---

8. Rosenmuller, *Scholia in Vetus Testamentum*, 110.

Christ at all! The authorities have designed new posters that have no need to take Christ's birth into account. It seems to me that we are trying to rob Jesus of His time here on earth. ACE and BCE still have their starting point at the birth of Jesus, we just don't say so. The plan must be to hide it long enough so that the next generation comes to accept ACE and BCE as normal and don't equate them with Christ's birth. Though I must say the spirit of the anti-Christ in the world is on the losing side.

Psalm 45:17 tells us that God will perpetuate the name of Jesus through all generations. It has been decreed, and the name of Christ will be made known to each generation one way or another. Christmastime is a perfect example. God has made it fun, yet everyone gets to think about the birth of Jesus. People don't want to give up the giving of presents, the feasting, and the holiday time, but the one goes with the other. I know there are many ways in which Christmas is corrupted, but the enemies of Jesus can't remove the "perpetuation" of the remembrance of His birth so their next best line of attack is to twist the celebrations to their own end. Each Christmas it is important that true believers get out there into the community and sing carols. It is part of the decree of Psalm 45:17, "I will perpetuate your memory through all generations; therefore, the nations will praise you for ever and ever."

We give Jesus the praise He deserves just as the angels did on that first Christmas night. Heaven's inhabitants are still praising God, now it's our turn to join them. It's fitting and good that the upright should praise Him. It is a great feeling to do the right thing and lifting Jesus higher is the right thing.

7

A Life of Praise

Sometimes people start conversations with, "Do you know what they've done now?" It could be a stranger at the bus stop or someone you are waiting in line with, but whoever says it immediately puts pressure on the listener to answer, "No, what have they done now?" It seems like an innocuous question until you realize that "they," whoever "they" may be, are in for a large dose of searing hot criticism. Other people will even start with, "Do you know what the idiots have done now?" It's a loaded question. If I reply by saying, "No, what have they done now?" it means I am agreeing from the outset that "they" are indeed fools. A lady once started a conversation with me to that effect about her managers at work. Maybe the lady had a legitimate complaint, but it could be that her employers made a genuine decision for the good of the company and it somehow infringed upon the lady's set routine or comfort.

Jesus said, "Who appointed me a judge or an arbiter between you?" (Luke 12:14) and refused to get entangled in the affairs of two brothers. Paul told Timothy that some people are gossips and busybodies who say things they ought not to (1 Tim 5:13). It's easy to become an accomplice in tale bearing. The person being maligned is not there to present their side of the story. Proverbs 18:17 says, "The first to present his case seems right, until another comes forward to question him." The sinful mind thinks that if we can put someone else down it lifts us higher. What benefit is there in telling me anyway? Am I in a position to do something about it? If I were in a position of authority and could help or do something about the situation, then telling me may be justified, but that is not often the case. I have to protect my own heart, as told in Proverbs 4:23, for my heart is the wellspring of life. We take all kinds of evil into our minds through no fault of our own, but when I have a choice, I would rather not hear what "the stupid fools" have been up to. Sufficient for the day is my own stupidity without taking anyone else's on board. We're not supermen and superwomen and once innocence is soiled, it's not easy to forget what we've been told.

If I have a chicken and mushroom pie in the fridge for lunch, then realize it is three days past the use-by date, but eat it anyway because there's no other food in the house, my body will let me know. Proverbs tells us that the words of a gossip are like choice morsels, they go down to a man's inmost parts. If you listen to gossip, your spirit will let you know you've taken something on board that is alien to your frame. God didn't design us for evil; it affects us badly, so badly that it will kill us if left unattended. If your toe has gangrene, cut it off or infection will affect your whole body. If your ears hanker after tittle-tattle and tales of other people's misdemeanors, cut them off. Don't hang around with friends you know put other people down. Speak out in someone's defense if they are being given a hard time and are not there to defend themselves. Look for the good. There is usually something positive to say about people. We all do bad things and who could stand if God kept an account of our sins? If we forgive those who trespass against us, we keep ourselves free from the corruption that is in the world. The out-of-date chicken and mushroom pie will poison my body; the stories of a talebearer will poison my soul. Righteousness is a way of life. We teach our ears not to listen, and in the same way, we teach our eyes not to look.

God wants us to live in peace, yet peace is such a rare quality in the world. My mother used to have a top loading washing machine and when I was a child I would pull myself up on tiptoes and look inside. It was full of water, beautiful still water. But, in the middle of the water was a big plastic shaft with blades on it called an agitator. When my mother turned the power on, the agitator began to turn and churn up the water. I looked on amazed. Satan is an agitator; he wants to stir things up in our lives. God wants to lead us beside still waters to restore our souls. That is God's heart towards us. Heaven wants to help us; hell wants to harm us. Without wood a fire goes out; without gossip a quarrel dies down (Prov 26:20). Satan will provide fuel for the fire if you want it; he's the master at stirring things up. You can listen to him and his friends here on earth—those who love scandal, hearsay, and rumors—but there is a price to pay. We cannot listen to a scandalmonger and have peace as well. We have to choose.

Someone once phoned and started telling me something I didn't want to hear. I was thinking, "Oh no, don't tell me this. I've got Satan off me today; I don't want any of his demons latching onto me and sucking all the goodness out of me like leeches." Then the guy on the phone said, "Do you know what I mean?" I didn't answer him; so he said it again. I still didn't answer. Finally he changed the subject. I was left feeling glad I hadn't encouraged and added more fuel to the fire.

Of course, this is blinding light to many in the world; it is strong medicine not many can or would want to take it. However, the command of Scripture is, "Don't give the devil a foothold" (Eph 4:27). Christ Himself held His peace when lies were being told in Herod's presence (Luke 23). When dealing with contentious people we are warned to watch ourselves or we also may be tempted (Gal 6:1). Fire has a way of spreading and it could be us who are set ablaze.

The domain of darkness is a thick web of intrigue, lies, and deceit. The corridors of hell descend in a maze of self-righteous, holier than thou, plotting, pride, and prejudice. How can anyone escape? In *The Divine Comedy*, Dante's ever decreasing circles of hell may hold more truth than we realize. Within the series of three works (*The Inferno, The Purgatorio,* and *The Paradiso*) written between 1308 and 1321, Virgil guides Dante through the nine circles of Hell. The circles are concentric, each new one representing further and further evil, culminating in the center of the earth, where Satan is held, bound. Each circle's sin is punished in fashion fitting their crime: the sinner is afflicted by the chief sin he committed.[1]

I can see that part of the reason for listening and maybe joining in with defamatory conversations is our concern not to appear unfriendly or standoffish. Society's common ground for communicating is largely negative. If you doubt the veracity of that, and I could be wrong, read the newspapers, listen to snippets of conversations of people passing by, or watch the media interview some unsuspecting interviewee. Modern conversations tend to descend unless someone has something to sell, then the direction is upward, since positive talk is needed. We talk-up a product, but talk-down real life. It is the language of the world. C. S. Lewis commented:

> The humblest, most balanced and capacious minds, praised most, while the cranks, misfits and malcontents praised least, i.e. the healthy and unaffected man, even if luxuriously brought up and widely experienced in good cookery, could praise a very modest meal: the dyspeptic

---

1. Dante, *The Divine Comedy*, 67.

and the snob found fault with all. Praise almost seems to be inner health made audible.[2]

It is worthwhile having a "positive policy" when talking to people whose only intent seems to be to blacken someone's character or give their personal pessimistic philosophy of what is going on in their church, street, home, or workplace. It is an objective that does not always work but it keeps my own soul from being stained. Outside a retirement home where I'd gone to sing, I asked a man how he was doing.

"Not very well," came the reply. He said he didn't like it there. I asked him several questions and got a negative reply to every one.

"How is your family?"

"They never come to see me."

"What, never?"

"No, never . . . they only came to see me twice last week."

So then I said, "Well, how about coming inside to listen to the gospel, everyone else is coming in; the gospel can change us."

At which he looked up at me and said, "I'm glad you've come."

I thought I'd broken through his hard exterior and then he added, "'Cause they need changing in there."

I couldn't break through the hardness. It's a sad story of someone in the grip of the devil's devices. He has hope in that he is still alive; while there is life, there is hope. If he could let go of the bitterness long enough for some peace to seep into his heart, then the floodgates may open. If only something could be done, however drastic, to stop him looking inward with cold hatred for life. If he could pry the door of his heart open for a few moments and feel the love

---

2. C. S. Lewis, *Reflections on the Psalms*, 80.

of God, like air rushes into a vacuum when a sealed door is opened, then it would surely stay open for eternity. Satan's work is to keep the door shut; he heaps all kind of resentments, bitterness, and unforgiveness behind it, making it hard for anyone wanting to get the door opened from the outside. It is hard even for the person to whom the door belongs to make his way through the rubble and actually open it. He is a prisoner of his own making, living in squalor unable to move, hemmed in by his own sin until there is so much debris that he can't even see that there is a door to be opened. Some people acquiesce to the despair, thinking this is the way life has been and always will be. Any romantic ideals they once held in their youth of happiness, faithfulness, and love have long been buried under memories of unfaithful lovers, fair-weather friends, and personal pride.

We know, as Holman Hunt's painting portrays, the handle to the door is on the inside. No man or celestial agent can turn it, except the man to whom it belongs. Holding a lantern, Jesus stands on the outside knocking on a closed door (Rev 3:20). If anyone else could turn it, the man to whom it belongs would not be a man. God is not willing that anyone should perish; it is our own will that does the damage.

One thing is certain: the door of any man's heart will not be opened with hearsay, gossip, and scandal. There are ways of winning over those people whose life's work is to exude doom and gloom, without us appearing unfriendly or confrontational. With God's help we will have a word in season for some lost soul, helping them toward the light. Proverbs 25:11 tells us "A word aptly spoken is like apples of gold in settings of silver." God has a big interest in the language we use. He created languages; He loves to see them used well. Communication is a gift. We watch plays and TV shows that communicate something to us; we enjoy the art of communication. From our earliest years, most of us have had stories read to us. It's a delight when communication is done well. God is a great communicator. Look at the Bible, it is concise and quite a short book considering its purpose. God tells us the things we need to know through engaging poetry, tales with twists and turns, and lessons from history. I've always loved reading the Scriptures. When we use words unwisely, without thought for those who hear them, it saddens God's heart. We are to avoid vain talk and godless chatter (1 Tim 6:20; 2 Tim 2:15). Every idle word we utter somehow accumulates and compounds our account into debit (Matt 12:36). The Bible also tells us not to curse. God gave language to the human race as a gift. It is not meant for confusion; God is not the author of confusion. Let your "yes" be "yes." Profanity is highlighted in the third commandment; language is not meant for swearing but for us to express our thoughts, not uncontrolled passion.

I found myself talking to a shopkeeper who told me a sorry tale of the futility of life, growing old, and having too few customers to meet his overhead. I replied by saying that our lives are like a mist. He gave me a quizzical look, so I explained to him that our days in the great scheme of things may be short, but we should live life in all its fullness. I continued to tell him that, like him, I have been self-employed for many years, but never worry about my income. God supplies all I need, leaving me to get on with the important things in life, including loving God and my neighbor, enjoying my wife and family, playing music, teaching children, going to church, etc. As we spoke, customers started coming into the shop and buying things. He carried on talking to me as he served them, and he began to laugh, saying there might be something in that, we've only been talking about it and things are looking up already. "Come back" he said, "And talk some more about God, if this is what happens."

God is full of good humor. Doesn't He who made the eye see? Doesn't He who made the ear hear? Doesn't He who gave us a sense of humor have one? Humor reflects joy, and Jesus has an abundance of joy. G. K. Chesterton said, "There was some one thing that was too great for God to show us when He walked upon the earth; and I have sometimes fancied that it was His mirth."[3]

Spreading God's love around can be fun; it's not the scary ordeal that we sometimes think it is. God wants us to have life in all its fullness, to float through life resting in Him, not to be stressed out. I spoke to two teenage girls on the street eating chips and they said they didn't believe in God. "You don't believe in God," I cried out, "but who made the potatoes for your chips?" It may not seem funny in print, but at the time with me a perfect stranger, we all ended up laughing. Humor is sometimes what is needed for a person to open up the door of their heart; God knows that and works with us. I was able to talk some more to the girls and leave them with some literature. C. S. Lewis said, "Joy is the serious business of heaven."[4] Helen M. Luke quotes T. S. Elliot who calls it *the laughter at the heart of things*.[5] We get so entangled in the cares of life that we hardly give God a chance to make us laugh. It is not God who has no sense of humor; sometimes it's us.

This doesn't mean that Christians are escapists—who more than Christians should be realists? We don't pretend that everything is fine in the world while whistling "Always Look On The Bright Side Of Life." We know we are fallen people in need of salvation, accept the deprivation of humankind, and understand that the universe is subject to entropy and decay. However, we also know that space and time is unfolding in a loving direction. Evil is not the force or power some people would have us believe. Evil is the absence of good, in the same way that darkness is the

3. Chesterton, *Orthodoxy*, 240.
4. Lewis, *Prayer: Letters to Malcolm*, 95.
5. Luke, *The Laughter at the Heart of Things*.

absence of light. Evil is a hole, a gap, and those who ally themselves with it are futilely trying to resist the flow of the river of life. Just like a man who might stand in an estuary trying to halt the surging waters flowing into the sea using only his arms and legs. Satan's evil schemes are an aberration of the daily journey towards goodness; wickedness is a hiatus that will come to an end. It may not seem that way at present because the devil knows his time is short and makes his presence felt. Each day is another page turned in the story of divine goodness where God is working all things together for those who love Him. We are living in what the Bible calls "the old order of things" (Rev 21:4). When the new order of things comes, the old order will seem like a far and distant memory. In the spectrum of eternity, evil will look like a tiny minuscule blip on the distant horizon looking over our shoulder from where we have come. The longer eternity is, the smaller evil becomes; we won't even bring the former things to mind. "Behold I will create new heavens and a new earth. The former things will not be remembered, nor will they come to mind" (Isa 65:17).

Some people say, "No one asked me if I wanted to be born." Well, maybe this life is the asking. Do you want to be born? Born again? Born of the spirit? Flesh and blood cannot inherit the kingdom of God. The human frame must be changed to go into the new universe and we have a choice to make. The body we have at present was made from this universe; it belongs here. God made the human body first, then breathed spirit into it. In the new order of things, the spirit will come first, then the body. The new spirit we have will generate a first class body. At present, we have a body to house the spirit and soul. Then, we will have a spirit and soul that clothes itself with body. It won't be the kind of flesh we know here—flesh that ails, gets sick, and tires—but a body like Christ's resurrected body. Not limited by the confines of the old order of things, but a powerful body and an eternal body. "This is the grand design of providence, and the end to which all events must tend."[6]

Death and decay have already started to reverse, with the resurrection of Jesus and the first fruits. The kingdom of God is like yeast that a woman took and mixed into a large amount of flour until it worked all through the dough (Luke 13:20). The large amount of dough can be thought of as what philosophers call "the whole show," or the complete system of things. The yeast, in this instance, is goodness that will work its way through heaven and earth. Sin and the old order of things will burn and shrivel up, never to be seen again. Satan's domain is divided against itself and will not stand (Mark 3:24), and like the Gerasenes swine, will destroy itself (Mark 5:13). Dante's hell gets smaller and smaller the further into it someone goes. Heaven gets larger and larger, and the further into it you get, the more you realize there is to discover because God is big, so big we'll never come to the end of Him. Hell is small because those for whom it was designed are small, small-minded, petty, and full of mischief. The hell in C. S. Lewis' book *The Great Divorce* was almost nothing. The "shades" in hell did not get to see heaven by travelling to it, but by growing larger.[7] I think it was Shakespeare who said all characters must shrink or widen. John Paul II delivered a similar sentiment, "People grow or diminish in moral stature," in a sermon at the Feast of Saint Francis de Sales in 2004. We become either small-minded or big-hearted, resist the Holy Spirit or submit to His will, and our humanity diminishes or we grow in grace.

The fruit of the Spirit is the direction in which the river of life is flowing. Those going against the current will be left behind, ultimately becoming the residue of what a human being used to be. In Dante's *The Inferno*, Virgil is

---

6. Spurgeon, *Spurgeon's Devotional Bible*.
7. Lewis, *The Great Divorce*, 112.

asked if he is a man and he replies, "No, but I once was a man."[8] Dante called those in hell "shades" for they had no real substance left to them, because that is the decision they made on earth. They refused to be people of substance; they had no moral fibre and were blown about by whichever way the evil wind of change blew them. With no honor, no character, and reaping what they have sown, they now have no substance. All that is left is their bitterness, hatred, selfish ambition, and pride, which rumble on like an infernal machine. All that made them human—their ability to love, create, enjoy, and praise—has disappeared, leaving the faint resemblance of what a human being used to be.

Mechanics sometimes say that a rubber joint has perished in a car engine, and when they extract it, it looks nothing like it used to. It is jagged and frayed, no longer able to do the job for which it was intended. Jesus said it is better to lose a hand or an eye than to perish. God made us for a purpose: to be Human, to live, love and enjoy God. Those in hell have resisted that purpose and are unable to enjoy and therefore to praise; they will be a sad shadow of a human being. Jesus didn't say without reason, "Fear Him who is able to destroy both body and soul in hell" (Matt 10:28). If what they had become on earth was a poor reflection of what God intended a human being to be, even what they have here will be taken from them (Matt 13:12).

In the children's story *"The Snow Queen,"* a small shard from the cold queen's broken mirror would bury itself into her victim.[9] The coldness from the shard would work its way throughout the entire person, until there was no warmth left at all. Hence, to praise anyone or anything was out of the question and therefore, to enjoy anything was also impossible. But while there is the slightest little bit

---

8. Alighieri, *The Divine Comedy*, 67.
9. Frank and Frank, *The Stories of Hans Christian Andersen*.

of warmth left in a person, God will try to encourage that warmth to spread. He won't break a bruised reed; nor will he snuff out a smouldering wick (Isa 42:3). As long as there is the slightest image of God flickering in a person, it will be encouraged to burst into flame and shine its light. "As when juice is still found in a cluster of grapes and men say, 'Don't destroy it, there is yet some good in it'" (Isa 65:8).

We need to take the greatest care to protect our own hearts. "Above all else protect your heart for it is the wellspring of life" (Prov 4:23). The imagery of Scripture is often severe; Jesus spoke of cutting off parts of our body (Matt 5:29–30). Psalm 137:8–9 (GNB) says, "Happy is the man . . . who takes your (Babylonian) babies and smashes them against a rock." When someone we know hurts us, maybe a friend or family member or someone we work with or go to church with, we need to take care because something sinister could be growing within us. We may not realize what it is at first, except for a reluctance to carry on from where we left off with that person. The next time we see them our greeting has none of its usual warmth; we no longer feel the need to invite them for coffee or ask how they are. At some point it happens to us all. We all have a little Babylonian baby in our arms, and we can choose to feed it by nursing the grudge, or strangle it by turning the other cheek and being warm, friendly, and forgiving to those who have trespassed against us. Little babies grow; so does sin. What starts out as a feeling of bitterness can, if something isn't done about it, end up as a permanent lodger eating all the goodness we have within us. We have all heard of brothers, cousins, and even children and parents who refuse to have anything to do with each other. Years go by in which not a word is exchanged. In some cases they can't even remember what the argument was that parted them in the first place. Babylonian babies grow into despotic tyrants that grow far larger than their host, taking over the leadership of their lives. Where love should guide, hatred now makes the decisions. Where grace would cover up an offense, anger now dictates behavior. Warmth is replaced by coldness; enjoyment has long gone, and light leaves the eyes. That's why Scripture teaches us to show sin no mercy. When infantile resentment takes its first gasp of air, we must beat the little brat's brains in. Don't let it live in your house. When vice is young, it is at its weakest, hence Jesus said, "Turn the cheek" (Matt 5:39). Don't let it go any further, don't let it grow; it is much harder to bind the strong man than to overcome a baby.

We must not let the coldness spread; we need to be warm, open, and humble. It's so easy to get cynical as we grow older, to develop a "we've seen it all before" attitude. Is that one of the reasons why God reduced man's years on earth? How did those before the flood cope? At 900 years old, were they still excited about life? There was more chance to repent, but more chance to grow bitter. God knows the best way of leading us to repentance—something He is trying to do with each one of us. "As the tree falls so shall it lie," says Ecclesiastes 11:3. When a tree has been cut down, it has done all the growing it's going to do. If it has grown diseased, diseased it will remain. If a piece of furniture were made from it, the furniture would be substandard and not fit for its purpose. If it has fallen to the north or to the south, it cannot move itself; the state in which we die, we will remain. It is not that God couldn't change it if He wanted to; it's the way it is. We will have become what we are.

Those who are becoming like Christ are able to praise, whatever the circumstances. Remember Laura? She was a vivacious five-year-old who caught the world's attention by her courage in the face of adversity. Unable to digest food, the little girl from Greater Manchester travelled to New Jersey where she underwent a successful liver and bowel transplant. A short year later, she was admitted to a Pennsylvania hospital where the most ambitious multi-organ transplant—liver, bowel, kidneys, stomach, and pancreas—was attempted. Little Laura died in November 1993, though doctors reported that she almost made it. Laura's parents were interviewed on TV shortly after her death and showed no signs of bitterness, only signs of thanksgiving and celebration for Laura's short life. They were grateful that God had brought five years of happiness into their lives, telling the interviewer that God had now taken her to be with Himself.

Those who know that God is good see all things from the vantage point of thankfulness; it is quite a high mountain where you are able to see for some way. The unthankful can't see very far at all, because ungratefulness is a pit where the disgruntled sit and groan about no one asking their permission if they wanted to be born. The thankless and selfish will get their wish; nothing of value will come their way. The rich man in Hades didn't even have a drop of water. The words of Jesus were, "Whoever has, will be given more, and he will have an abundance. Whoever does not have, even what he has will be taken from him" (Matt 13:12).

Praise is intrinsically linked to heaven, while selfishness is an integral part of hell. If we are thankful in adverse circumstances, it adds to our treasure in heaven. Being ungrateful compounds the misery of hell. The virtue we have on earth will be commensurate with the treasure we have in heaven. The vice we cling to here is also commensurate with the torment of hell. As Jesus said, some will be beaten with many blows and some with few (Luke 12:47–48).

"Let your conversation always be full of grace, seasoned with salt," said the Apostle Paul (Col 4:6). We need a healthy sprinkling of thankfulness and praise in our conversations and life.

8

Creative Praise

THE WELL-ESTABLISHED review section of magazines and websites informs us that there is a good percentage of people who enjoy reading them—reviews of music, books, plays, movies, and a host of other things too. If you are thinking of purchasing a car, it's worth while reading a review of the car. To be sure, it is only one man's opinion, but if he does his job well, the review will be informative and help towards your decision of whether to buy the car or not. Reviews give us inside information from someone familiar with the art of critique. Music reviews, for instance, have an important role. They help push the standard of music higher; a sharp reviewer soon pounces upon sloppiness. Artist and Repertoire (A & R) people have to give a critical appraisal of a singer or band to the record company they work for. The company executives will, on the word of the A & R person, invest money in a particular artist.

For the last seventeen years I have been asked to review music for *CrossRhythms* magazine and website. I approach the task with both enthusiasm and a sense of responsibility. Firstly, enthusiasm, because listening to the music is enjoyable and it's nice to know someone thinks my opinion may be worth something. I suppose we are all reviewers in some way. Coming home from a football match, people jam the phone lines of their local radio station in an attempt to give their opinion of how the game went. Listening to the comments people make, I realize that we all make similar comments about hundreds of different things everyday, things as diverse as concerts, washing machines, and even sermons at church.

Secondly, my responsibility stems from the fact that my review may cause people to part with their money and buy the CD. It also stems from the negative experience of my own music being the subject of a bad review. The CDs I have released have received many reviews. It is disconcerting, even grim, to read a bad one and can affect you for some time. By bad, I do not mean a review that has constructive criticism to offer, but one that is written with a general tone of cynicism by a journalist with some sort of grudge. It is an easy temptation to fall into; we make good armchair judges, lifting ourselves higher as we put someone else down.

Giving praise has the opposite effect; it causes us to lower ourselves so someone else may be lifted. The sense of responsibility is heightened when I read James, who says, "Not many of you should presume to be teachers, my brothers, because you know that we who teach will be judged more strictly" (Jas 3:1). However, it does fall to some to become teachers. My English teacher at school would read through my essays and give them a critical analysis, awarding me marks out of ten. There is a place for the well-balanced critic, for someone who knows their subject, passes on their knowledge as servants, and demonstrates respect for both the people whose work they review, and those who will read it.

The danger, of course, lies in thinking we are all great critics able to offer an opinion on nearly every subject. It is certainly off-putting to any prospective writers, singers, or artists. The reluctance of young people to show their artwork may be something to do with their youth, but also partly out of fear of criticism. Fox TV's reality show *American Idol* gave us all the chance to laugh at other people's off-key singing; it is part of the show's appeal. Maybe that is why the people in a previous chapter were reluctant to sing "*Happy Birthday.*"

Getting heckled and criticized is, I suppose, part and parcel of learning to perform in front of people. The artist is, after all, a servant and performing can be a humbling experience, and so it is good for the performer to be humble to begin with. Many singers and bands have come unstuck trying to keep up a non-existent image. As a seventeen-year-old, in one of my first concerts, my guitar strap broke. I only just managed to catch the guitar before it crashed into the floor. The audience thought this was funny; I didn't. I began to learn fast that being lowly to begin with could save a lot of embarrassment later on. The good thing about being humble is that you don't get embarrassed; you don't have to pretend you are perfect. You're a human being who makes mistakes, just like everyone else. Christ humbled Himself to the death on a cross, "I am a worm not a man," cries out the prophetic Psalm 22. The word "humble" comes from the Latin word *humus*, which means the ground. Worms crawl around in the ground. Christ was lowly of heart; He came from heaven to earth, then below the earth in the tomb, and through the resurrection and ascension, was lifted high. Those who humble themselves will be lifted, but those who are proud will be brought low.

Being humble is not something we can shout about. If someone gives you a badge saying that you are humble, don't wear it. Ask the Lord for humility, but don't thank Him for it. I'm not so sure we should pray, "Lord keep me humble." Maybe we should pray, "Lord make me humble" and "Lord somehow help me to have a humble heart, help me to show the humility of Christ." The Lord will help you and send along instances where you would normally be nothing but embarrassed, but now you can thank Him for helping you to be humble.

Creative Praise 77

I was asked to sing at a golf conference and accepted the invitation. Then, the organizer asked me if I could play golf. I said, "yes" and he put my name down for 18 holes of golf. When the day came I said "hi" to a few of the other players and took a few practice swings. I noticed that official-looking people were staring at me, then one of them approached and told me that I couldn't play golf in a T-shirt, as it was against the club's rules. "You can only play in a shirt with a collar," he said. One of the other golfers very kindly said he had a spare shirt, which did have a collar on it; he would be happy to loan it to me if I wanted. I did want, and hurried away to find somewhere I could change into the proper shirt.

At the first tee there was a group of onlookers gathering to see everyone's opening shots. The shots were all pretty good, and the people watching made an assortment of approving noises. Then came my turn. I hit the ball hard; the ball skewed at a tangent into some bushes about seventeen meters away. I had to walk over to them and find the ball, because the next golfer couldn't tee off until I'd found it. Those few meters seemed like a long walk; my neck started to get strangely hot under my newly acquired collar. The crowd of onlookers went strangely quiet. I searched for the ball but was unable to find it, which meant I lost points for the team I had been allocated to and then I had to tee off again. The second shot dribbled onto the fairway but was at least on the fairway. By this time all I was thinking was a mixture of "eek" and "thank You Lord for another opportunity to be humble." The Lord seems to send along these excellent opportunities to be humble because He is shaping us to be like Christ, helping us to lose our ideas of self-importance.

Pray "Lord make me humble" and watch the great opportunities He sends your way. Furthermore, I do believe that these tests in humility get a little easier to bear with each successive trial. Recently, I went mountain biking with a group of cyclists; it was my first time with them and some of the maneuvers were quite tricky. One particular steep downhill section was very precarious and each person attempted it in turn. Everyone received hoots and hollers as they successfully negotiated it. I was last in line and there was a lot of shouting for me to let go and go with the flow of the downhill pull. Halfway down the hill I began to fall off my bike quite spectacularly in going . . . going . . . gone fashion. I tried to pull my bike back on course but couldn't manage it and had to let gravity do its worst. The shouting reached a joyous crescendo as I hit the ground. As I picked myself up out of the mud, I again thanked God for another opportunity to be humble. Lots of faces seemed to be looking at me but I noticed I felt a lot better about this than when I sliced the golf ball. I don't think I'm humble yet, in fact I am sure I'm not, but God is working with me and taking me in that direction with each successive lesson. (A little later after my fall someone else fell off their bike and they landed in a stream. That made me feel a little better too, although I'm sure not for the right reasons.)

Whether we are preaching, singing praises, or performing, we have to lose any pretense we may have and put ourselves totally into the art of communicating—forgetting what others might think and what the critics will say. If we want to engage others, we ourselves have to be engaged. We are not guaranteed to reach those who hear, but at least we give ourselves the best chance. John Wesley sometimes remarked that he would sing and preach with all his heart to some congregations, but could find no way to reach the people. That is sometimes true, but it's the exception and not the rule.

I was asked to sing in a Sunday morning service at a certain prison. One of the inmates came over to me just before the start of the service and said, "Everyone was bored with the singer that they sent to us last week." I thanked him for the warning and proceeded to tell the men the story of how I learned to play the guitar as a young boy in church. My friends and I would stay behind after church to secretly practice all the songs we had heard on the radio. If for some reason the pastor came back into the church, the rock music we were playing would suddenly turn into the country and western hymn *This Little Light Of Mine*. To illustrate this to the prisoners, I sang a Rolling Stones song. I sang it with all my heart coming close to the gusto and energy Mick Jagger himself puts into the song. This was most unusual for the inmates who seemed to be enjoying themselves. My motive, like Wesley, was to move my hearers. It is easy for some people to get hemmed in by a tough-guy macho image. I thought if I could get some of these men to show some interest in the music I play, it would be a breakthrough. I sang the Stone's tune knowing in my heart that I did it to the Lord. I could see the prisoners nodding along to the rhythm. They listened attentively, not only to the Stone's song, but also to my own songs and everything I had to say about Jesus. Afterwards men came to me to shake my hand and talk to me. The warden on duty said, "That's the first time I have seen the men respond in a chapel service and listen in silence without heckling."

To be demonstrative can be hard for some people, whether it is raising a hand in a church service or acting out a gospel drama on the street. It will, however, bear fruit if we do it with all our hearts to the Lord, in our own lives if not anyone else's. Colossians 3:23 says, "Whatever you do, work at it with all your heart, as working to the Lord." It's important to be humble and not worry about what other people will think, but do what we do to the Lord.

There is a time for critique, but being critical is not always good; it can easily become a way of life. There's a danger of nothing being sacred; everything is up for grabs. We become critical of almost everything we encounter, hard to please, and in the end, a cynical person. It's not a happy state to be in, plus it may hinder tender hearts that have yet to burst into bloom. It grieves me when I hear children being put down by their parents. I heard one dad telling his son that the boy's ability to play football was rubbish. But that's not the point. If the son enjoys football, he should be encouraged to play it, whatever his ability. It is great exercise and who knows, he may go on to learn a few tricks, get stronger, faster, and go on to play for a local team. But even if he never goes on to excel, the main point is that it's fun! Fathers should be happy that their children are having fun. It also helps them to be team players, which is so important in life.

When we judge people's efforts, especially in church, we fall into the enemy's hands. It is a bit like the end of a cooking program on TV where judges prod and poke the dinner that has just been laid out, and test the standard of cooking by eating a tiny amount of it. They are then able to give a critical assessment of the chef's ability. But, unless they eat the food, they won't get any benefit from it. We gather at church to receive what God has for us. If He, in His wisdom, has chosen a particular brother or sister to bring a word of exhortation, it is for us to receive it with thanksgiving. Welsh poet George Herbert said it is not us who judge the preacher but the preacher who judges us. The wind of the Spirit blows where it will, and so it is with those who are born of the Spirit. We cannot see the wind blowing, and neither can we see whom God's Spirit is blowing through. It may be blowing through the person preaching, but the spiritual meal being served up is of little value to us because we are making a mental critique of his sermon and thinking, "I hope we've got lasagne for dinner." After church, back home we are delighted to see that we do in fact have lasagne for dinner and the preacher for dessert.

It's so important that we receive what God has for us, whoever His messenger may be. I have been to many types of church services on my travels and have always found that if I seek God, He will be found whatever type of service it may be. When we sit around the Sunday afternoon dinner table it is so easy to give the messenger a hard time. "What did you think of the sermon today?" Just asking it seems like a loaded question. "Well he was quite wrong about Armageddon you know, the next time he gets up to preach armageddon outta there!" There is, of course, a place for testing sound doctrine and it is important that Scripture is the standard. But, what usually seems to take place under the guise of "testing for sound doctrine" is an invitation for a critical spirit to get to work. True praise that God enjoys must surely be people who meet with humble hearts ready to receive what He gives that day, whoever His servant may be. He may use someone to plant good seeds that day but the ground is not broken; it still needs ploughing and the seed fails to take root in our lives. Surely God knows what we need; His divine providence has made sure that we are within earshot of what that brother or sister has to say. We may not have a palate for it; the preacher may not have the art of communication at his fingertips, but if we listen, there will be food in there for us from our Father.

Sometimes we are at a church where the preaching seems like hard going; it may mean we have to eat manna for a while. Manna isn't the most appealing food but it is nutritious and strengthens those who eat it. In countries where food is scarce, people are willing to eat any food that comes their way. In the west where food abounds, we pick, choose, and get fat. It is a similar thing in church. We have many good teachers these days that are able to communicate well and when we have someone from our own congregation it may for hard for us to receive from him.

For two reasons it is not always easy to receive teaching from people in our congregation. The first is that we know them. Jesus said a prophet has no honor in his own hometown (Matt 13:57). Yet, God can deposit some good gift in one of our neighbors, friends, or family members and we can be tempted not to acknowledge the gift because God chose to give them the gift and not us. "Why him and not me?" we question, while failing to realize that God may have given us a completely different gift. The second reason is that we have heard good communicators on TV, and it's probably fair to say that some of the people who preach to us at church lack the same skill of communication. This doesn't mean they don't have any valid points to make or that God can't use them, but it does mean that congregants have to apply themselves to listening, and that isn't the easy option. Some are tempted to stay at home and watch the preachers on TV, or just watch TV instead of going to church. But God wants us to meet together; it's important to Him and important for us to have fellowship.

God has made us gregarious for a reason. We learn from one another as the Holy Spirit reveals things to different members of our local church. Maybe God is teaching us more than just what the preacher is saying. Perhaps we are learning to apply ourselves to righteousness by getting an opportunity to grow in grace, exercise patience, and develop a willing heart. It is sweet praise in God's ears when our worship extends past the "time of praise and worship" we give Him in meetings.

Another danger in expressing critical comments is that the young and recently converted may hear and become fearful of being asked to share what God has given them. When I was about 12 years old and in a youth group, I played my guitar in a church we were visiting and a guy from that church came up to me after our song and said, "Did you know your guitar was out of tune?" I really didn't need to hear that at that particular moment. Nowadays I would just say, "Hey, that's rock 'n' roll," but back then it was harder to take. It didn't put me off playing and singing, but the last thing a young person in church or a recent convert needs to hear are comments like, "Well, his guitar was out of tune, but he had a go didn't he? You have to admire him for that." Or, "She's not really an actor but it was a nice sketch for the children, don't you think?" Or, "I can tell he's been to Bible college, but he's got to make his preaching a lot more interesting if he wants to keep my attention." It is condescending and enough to dampen the enthusiasm of any prospective young person even trying to do something creative. It also loses the main objective of what is going on: that God may have spoken to the listeners through the faltering lips of the people singing, acting, or preaching. God uses the weak things of the world to overcome the strong, and He chooses the foolish things of world to confound the wise (1 Cor 1:27).

A friend of mine, who has been a Christian singer/songwriter for some years, told me he sometimes wonders about the comments people make to him after a concert. We have both had people approach us (this is true of preaching, too) who seemed to think that the songs that were sung and any talk in-between them was not for them at all, but for others in attendance. Even though they sat in the audience, they didn't seem to consider themselves a part of it. They offer their opinion on how the show went and give tips on how it could be improved to win the approval of the audience. My friend makes me laugh by coming up to me after I've performed and says, "Oh, Paul, if you could have only stood on your head and juggled for just a few minutes longer while drinking a glass of milk, I think you would have really won the audience over." When we sit in a Christian audience or congregation, we are a part of it. The songs, sermon, and anything else that happens, is aimed at us and for our enjoyment or edification. We are an integral part of what God is doing in that particular gathering. It may be that our job is to receive or possibly to give, but we cut ourselves off when we adopt the position of onlooker.

> Judge nothing before the appointed time; wait till the Lord comes. He will bring to light what is hidden in the darkness and will expose the motives of men's hearts. At that time each will receive his praise from God." (1 Cor 4:5)

Being a critic can be habit forming, it spreads throughout our life, just like fungi in a bowl of fruit. A time may come when the critic becomes a critical person unable to receive ministry; compelled to give a running commentary on church like it's a football game on TV. If we don't receive good food, we will become malnourished, and may starve. I've been in church many years and have seen this scenario acted out. Someone starts walking with the Lord full of enthusiasm, ready and eager to learn from God, then people get in the way, and the convert's attention is diverted away from God and placed on people. He begins to disagree with certain things in the church, which is sometimes a valid thing. He may not be speaking untruth, but just because we are able to do it, doesn't mean we should. Satan loves to divide, but it is one of the things God hates. Proverbs 6:16 tells us there are six things that God hates, and one of them is a man who stirs up dissension among brothers. When we are told there is something God hates, we ought to listen. The sad thing is that new Christians sometimes learn how to grumble from watching older Christians do it. Jesus' prayer was that we may be one. So, before we pick that contentious subject to preach on or to talk about with our friends, let's remember Christ's prayer and stop to think whether our subject is going to bring Christians closer to each other or further away. Satan loves small things; he's the "master of minutia." Of course there are things wrong with our churches; they have people in them and people make mistakes. People are born to trouble. The church that has no problems is a church that has no people. Being a Christian means learning to forgive. It's good for us to let things pass, to turn the cheek, to let love cover over a multitude of sins.

Critical behavior belongs to the world and so does the fear of being criticized. Do not let the world squeeze you into its mold. The enemy of our souls has a stranglehold on our freedom of expression in much the same way as a boa constrictor slowly squeezes the life out of its prey. Christ has set us free from embarrassment so we can dance like no one is watching, sing like a bird in a tree, and praise God in freedom of expression.

Years ago, families created their own entertainment at home or at parties by playing instruments, singing, storytelling, and acting out plays they may well have written themselves. Times have changed; entertainment is piped into our homes from several directions. The need for us to create our own has diminished. People used to take time over the evening meal enjoying the art of conversation. Sitting in front of the TV eating dinner is sometimes fun, but it's better for the family to sit around a table catching up with what everyone has been doing and telling stories. It used to be that the majority enjoyed their own creativity, but now "the many" are entertained by "the few."

I remember at my own school, peer pressure hindered many creative children from displaying their talents. My son tells me that in the four schools he has attended, he is often the only boy who dances at the school parties. I can understand that some children are shy, but I also think it is a general move in society that boys are hindered from expressing themselves in dance. The boa constrictor is at work; Satan ensnares. The fear of man is a snare, but Christ sets us free.

When I go into secondary schools (ages 11–16) in the UK to sing and speak at assemblies, it is a shame, though not a surprise, to see that there is hardly any collective singing. When I attended school, singing in the assemblies was not good, to say the least, but now it's almost non-existent. I didn't help matters when I was a schoolboy but I'm grateful to God that He has graciously given me opportunities to go back into schools to sing to the students. I won't say it's easy, but now and again I get the children singing. A lot depends on the song itself, but it can be done, and when it works, it's a lot of fun. Satan wants to stifle people's creativity; if no one sings glory to God, then no one's heart can be stirred through singing.

I remember being at college talking to some fellow students as a teenager. I happened to illustrate a story with oral sound effects. After making one such noise, a lad who had been listening said, "How did it go?" I made the noise again and quickly realized that his intention in asking for the repeat was to cause embarrassment, not because he was interested in the story, but because he was interested in belittling me. The inhibiting influence of darkness again reared its ugly head. If making theatrical sound effects to enhance a story gives a young student the appearance of a buffoon, he will soon cease to be theatrical. We all make interesting sounds as children. As I write this, my son is going through the house making dush-dish-dish noises to illustrate a game he is playing. I had never seen someone shown up for making sound effects; it seemed to be a new thing when I was at college. I've since heard it quite a few times. Some people think it is fun to make sport of someone else, I've even heard Christians say it.

There will be people who scoff, we can be pretty sure of that, but the freedom we have in Christ means we don't need to be inhibited to praise, sing, or express ourselves. King David danced before the Lord with all of his strength, wearing a minimum of clothing to allow him maximum movement. His wife, Michal, watched him from an upstairs window and despised him. When David returned home, she sarcastically commented, "How the king of Israel distinguished himself today, disrobing in the sight of slave girls as a vulgar fellow might do" (2 Sam 6:20). David replied, "Before the Lord I will celebrate, and I am prepared to become even more undignified than that" (2 Sam 6:22). On the day David stands before God and is asked what he did with his strength, one of the things he will be able to say is, "Lord, I danced for You." David's dance has been recorded for us here on earth, but not only on earth is it recorded; it will shine for all eternity as a treasure in David's account.

Psalm 33:3 tells us to play skillfully and make a loud noise. It tells us to do this because creativity reaches the human heart. Sometimes women (and men) cry while watching a film because the acting, story, and music have touched them. When we lift Jesus higher, it will touch people. Some people will turn away, but there are those who will be drawn. John the Baptist sang a dirge, but some wouldn't mourn; Jesus played the flute, but some wouldn't dance (Matt 11:17). But there are always those who will join in the dance and sing along. Music is one of the blessings God has put into the world because it can reach out and touch the hard heart of man.

I used to teach guitar in a music shop in Birmingham, England, where an older gentleman used to come for lessons. Early one morning just as the lesson was about to start, he asked me to play his guitar for him. It was a nice classical guitar that had been bought for him by his family. I asked what he wanted me to play and he replied by saying I could play anything, he just wanted to hear the guitar played nicely. So I played *Cavatina,* the theme from the movie *The Deer Hunter.* When I had finished playing, I looked up and saw that he had tears in his eyes. I couldn't think of anything to say, so while he tried to compose himself, I played another piece. When I finished the second piece, he was unable to continue with the lesson; he seemed truly broken. Before he left I mentioned that music is a powerful thing and that God speaks to us through it. It taught me something, too. I realized what an important place God has given music in the world. It is important that we play skillfully; we have to give God our best. That means practice. I'm sure God sees the practice we do as praise in itself; it shows that our heart is committed to giving Him the best. Jesus didn't actually play the flute (as far as we know) and John the Baptist didn't sing dirges. What Jesus is telling us is that God used all means—the full spectrum of blessings known to man—to reach our hard hearts. If we are going to play the flute then we can be certain that if it is not played well, it certainly won't win the hearts of the people. But if it is played well, it may. We have to use what God has given us for His glory.

The King James Version translates Psalm 107:8 as, "Oh, that men would praise the LORD." That's an interesting turn of phrase; why begin it with the word "Oh?" Why didn't the Psalmist say, "I would like it if men praised the LORD?" The New International Version translates Isaiah 44:23 as, "Sing for joy, O heavens, for the LORD has done this; shout aloud, O earth." Why not say, "You heavens, could you oblige me by shouting, and would you mind joining in earth?" The reason is that "Oh" or "O" is a cry from the heart, it's poetic and creative. As a free agent, God uses every means at His disposal to reach out to other free agents, and one of those means is poetry. We can choose to return His love or not, but we can see God's heart in what we read, He is revealing Himself in the poetry of Scripture. He holds nothing back but lets us know He loves us and yearns for us. He bares his soul as a young man may who tries to win the love of a girl. God jealously longs for the spirit that He made to live in us. His passion for our hearts reveals itself in Scripture. His Spirit in the hearts of His children makes us cry out with the same passion. If people smirk, laugh, or ridicule us, what does it matter? We must press on; love always perseveres. Spurgeon said, "If we decline from holiness because bad men laugh, we shall make good men weep."[1]

If the status quo continues in our young people, each successive generation will continue the descent into utilitarianism. Posterity need not sing, "Why should the devil have all the good music?" But, "Why hasn't the devil got any music?" He will paralyze all expressive action. The dictionary definition of the word "paralyze" is "an inability to act." How appropriate! Revelation 18:22 says, "The music of the harpists, musicians, flute players and trumpeters will never be heard in you again." Darkness is restrictive; the kingdom of light emancipates. Who the Son sets free is free indeed (John 8:36). Hell has no music, praise, or creativity and we can see its inhibiting affects here on earth.

> Nihilism cries out, "What's the point? We are vacant clouds of atoms blown around in a meaningless universe; let's get drunk."
>
> Materialism calls, "Amass possessions for yourself here on earth."
>
> Naturalism says, "We are animal, the species must survive."

The domain of darkness is too preoccupied with distrust, sensual indulgence, and survival to have any room for what Jesus called "life." It behooves us to use whatever talents we are given here on earth. The small talents we display here on earth may be infinitely increased in the age to come: the men who used their talents to good effect in the parable were given whole cities as their reward (Luke 19:17).

One of the marks of a good communicator is to behave as if his present audience is the most inspiring crowd he/she's ever performed before, however small and unresponsive they may be. When I have found myself with

1. Spurgeon, *Spurgeon's Devotional Bible*.

just a few people to sing to, I can feel the devil tugging at my shirtsleeves saying, "Why bother? Don't try too hard." I have to resist him and perform to the best of my ability. The people listening deserve to be treated with the best I can do. It is a privilege to have even one person listen to me; there are plenty of other things they could be doing. When I resist the devil and give it my best shot even though the audience is small, I've been surprised at the comments made to me afterwards. People tell me they soon forgot that there weren't many people there and how they experienced God's presence in a real way.

If God has placed something on our hearts, whatever it may be—a song, sermon, poem, dance, drama, creative act of worship, prayer, or spontaneous praise—we ought to do it as if we mean it, as if God is worth it, because He is. We should resist any fear of man. Why shouldn't God be praised? He should be, and it's important that He is praised. There is something intrinsically linked to life as we live it that demands good stories to be heard, praising God is telling people an excellent story. The universe declares it, the skies proclaim it, and there is no language where their voice is not heard (Ps 19:1–2). Human beings are a part of that same universe; we were taken from its dust and it is our duty to praise Him. If we don't praise God, even the very stones will cry out (Luke 19:40). The fear of man is an insidious snare, inhibiting us (Prov 29:25).

Sometime ago I went to town, and while I was walking along the street saw some street drama, which turned out to be performed by a group of Christians. As I watched I also noticed that a crowd gathered, in fact about 75% of people who were passing by took time to stop walking, put down their bags, and watch. It reminded me of John Wesley who would attract a crowd by singing and preaching in the marketplace of the town he was visiting. These days it's a lot harder to get people to take a street preacher seriously, so to see the Good News proclaimed by well-performed drama was great to see. I'm sure the Lord received it as a sweet smelling savor.

The Holy Spirit can use the smallest gesture: saying "God bless" at the end of a telephone conversation to an unbeliever may be hard for some people to say, but let's not quench the Spirit. It is praise to God when we let people know that He can and will bless them if they want Him to. It may seem emotional to introduce spiritual things into a conversation, but creativity affects our emotions. Even the hardest tough guy can be reached; he may have music that he likes to chill out to, or some other angle of creativity that he enjoys. We can connect with people by letting go of our inhibitions and being creative.

I have enjoyed telling people about the miracle that God did for my wife and me. I know some people really don't want me to talk to them about Jesus. I can tell quite easily, it's as if their shirt becomes suddenly itchy, they wriggle about in it. I know it is important to talk to people about a wide variety of subjects, which I enjoy doing, and I don't really want my neighbors thinking, "Oh no! Here comes Paul again to talk to me about God." But credit must be given where credit is due. Sometimes it's appropriate and fitting that God is given the glory He deserves even if our hearers get twitchy.

The medical profession told us that it was an impossible situation for me to become a father. Three different hospitals and consultants all said they couldn't help us. But what is impossible for man is possible for God. Our little boy is now ten. What an injustice if I do not tell what God has done for us because of the fear of man. Who do we fear more, or maybe another way of saying it is, who do we want to please more? It is fitting and right that the upright give God the glory He deserves (Pss 33:1, 147:1). Woe is me if I don't give glory where it is deserved. We must honor God in every way we can, and there are so many ways to honor Him. Some churches use kneeling, it is humbling to lower our body into a kneeling position. If you don't think so try it next time you are in a formal church setting. In the upwardly mobile western world there is a feeling that we must be up-standing. Some feel it is demeaning for someone to be on his or her knees like they are scrubbing the floor or something. But it is good for us to act out the scenario of who God is and who we are; it is He who made us and not we ourselves. It helps us to remember that we are in submission to Him and not He to us. We do not have to kneel, of course, but any opportunity to show God how we feel towards Him is a good one—and anyway, scrubbing the floor is a good thing.

He has asked us to love Him with all of our hearts, soul, and strength (Deut 6:5) and that is an amazing commandment; not "obey me" or "fear me," although we do those things, but "love me." Our heart is engaged in worship, not just our head. Using our body has a way of engaging the heart. Some churches encourage people to raise their hands; it is hard to raise your hands without your heart being engaged. You feel like too much of a fraudster to do it effectively. Raising your hands means engaging your heart. We can sing and be disinterested, listen to a sermon and be distracted, but raising your hands and being disinterested is a lot harder to do. In addition to kneeling and raising hands there are many ways of expressing praise, but whatever way we do it the Scriptures tell us to do it with all of our heart. That is what counts and it has a way of engaging others to do the same because creative praise encourages empathy. Empathy means "to be at one with the emotions of others," the dictionary definition includes "to lose oneself in a work of art." That's easy to see: when a film gets tense, we identify ourselves with the feelings of those in the story, they act out feeling fear and we feel the fear. We empathize with the emotions the people in the film are supposed to be feeling. In the film *Marathon Man*, where Dustin Hoffman is in the mad dentist's chair having his teeth drilled, who can watch that scene without having his own teeth set on edge? When we watch a footballer score a last minute goal after a strenuous, goalless 89 minutes, his creative act of punching the air somehow invites us to join him in his celebration. Even my wife who has little interest in football, if I can get her interested in a game, shouts, sings, and raises her hands in a victory salute when someone scores, just the way the players do.

We know that football teams often disappoint us, but when our victory salute is aimed towards Him who is never a disappointment, it takes on special value and encourages others to do the same. Our praises reach out not only to God but to those around us. That is what happened on the day of Pentecost: people heard the disciples praising God and about three thousand were added to their number that day. Men's consciences will be touched when they see others praising God, that they too ought to praise the Lord who is worthy to be praised. Paul said, "I want men everywhere to pray lifting up holy hands" (1 Tim 2:8). As we lift Jesus higher, He will draw all men to Himself.

It is a relief to lose the restriction put on us by the world and the fear of man, no one to answer to but Christ Himself. When I was a teenager, the youth leader at church asked me to take part in the Sunday evening service the young people had been asked to lead. It was my job to tell people how I became a Christian. I sweated and toiled over what to say for the three weeks leading up to the service. I began by saying, "I was brought up in a Christian home," which didn't surprise anyone because most of them had known me since I was born. Then a strange thing happened, I noticed that I wasn't a part of the congregation looking at the preacher but I was looking at the congregation and what was worse, they were looking at me. My brain decided to go into "can't think what to say" mode. I stood there for what seemed like a long time. I could have just legged it and got back into the congregation but somehow I managed to remain standing at the front until normal brain function was resumed. What hindered normal service being resumed was people saying, in voices just audible enough for me to understand, things like, "Bless him Lord" and "Help him Jesus." That didn't help me at the time, but I managed to utter a few more words to kind of sum things up and got out of the hot seat. I would have been the last choice for a communicator of the gospel had you been looking for one, but God has other plans and uses the weak things of the world to shame the strong (1 Cor 1:27).

Spurgeon said, "Let us rather stammer out Thy praises, than be entirely silent."[2] God often uses the despised things of the world to bring glory to His name. To show that He doesn't need man's strength, God is able all by Himself to do whatever He wants to do. I am in fact now a communicator of His Word. The prayers of "Help him Jesus" uttered by the well meaning people in church all those years ago have been answered, because Christ does help me to proclaim His word. If we are faithful in little, despite the cost to our self-esteem, the Lord knows we will also be faithful in much. Not too long after the youth service, I had my first real encounter with the Holy Spirit. What I had been trying to say with my head, I began to say with my heart. If we want to lift Jesus higher, our heart must be engaged.

Harold St. John's daughter wrote of an experience her father underwent that was too sacred to talk about and that "lifted him into a radiance and freedom he had never known before. The rather solemn, self-conscious holiness he had known before gave way to a sort of joy, as though he

---

2. Spurgeon, *Spurgeon's Devotional Bible*.

no longer had to watch his step in the heavenlies; he was at home there, self forgetful, absorbed in Christ."[3]

Some people think freedom is being totally selfish, doing what they want to do whether or not it inconveniences anyone else—let the flesh express what the flesh desires when the flesh wants to do it. In the kingdom of light, freedom means to let the flesh express what the Spirit desires, when the Spirit desires to do it. Inconveniencing people is not generally a good thing, but to walk in step with the Spirit may mean saying grace in a restaurant or praying with someone in a public place. This will not inconvenience other people—unless you are causing an obstruction—but it may cause other people to look at you, and the devil will use this as pressure on you not to bother praying. God can certainly use your prayer to convict the on-lookers that they too should pray, but the primary reason for following the Holy Spirit's lead is that it is the right thing to do. The fleshy mind, the mind concerned with the things of this world would cave in to such pressure as, "People might look at us." The Spirit makes us strong.

The Greek word for "belly" is "*koilia*," which comes from the word "hollow." Jesus uses *koilia* when He talks about rivers of living water coming from our belly. When air is pumped into a tire it is able to withstand being put on a car, bear the car's weight, and be driven at high speeds. Without pressurized air in it, it's a weak, floppy piece of rubber. Our human frame or belly is like a hollow that needs to be filled, and I don't mean filling it with food. Jesus used the word "belly" as a symbol. He spoke of our inner-man; the Holy Spirit fills our "hollow" and strengthens us, just like the air inside it strengthens the tire. We are then able to obey the leading of the Spirit, whatever that leading is.

---

3. St. John, *Harold St. John: A Portrait By His Daughter*.

In the past, people have used the phrase "being led" for doing exactly what they want to do, when in truth the Spirit leads us to do what He wants to do. Christ's love compels us, the compassion of Jesus overcomes our selfish inhibitions; we feel the feelings of Jesus and act accordingly. Because it is the Spirit of Jesus inside our hearts, we are one with Him. If someone needs prayer, we pray for them, and if in public is the only place we can do it then in public it shall be. God has filled our "hollow" and made us strong enough to call on Him wherever we may be. We have bodies and feelings that have a place in our lives, but the Spirit must come first. There is a time for everything under heaven and sometimes it is time to publicly call on God. If we follow the world's way, we are like the floppy piece of rubber without air, like animals who are hollow, and like horses that are flesh and not spirit. God created beasts bent over with a spine horizontal to the earth, with eyes that scan the plane of the earth. Human beings He created upright and able to look up at the stars, but since we have learned sin, we may be like animals, unable to lift our heads or hands. Those who follow the Spirit's leading have no such restrictions and are able to give full expression to creative praise.

Last week my wife, Lorraine, and I went to a restaurant. We met a friend of mine from the running club I belong to. His two daughters were with him and when he asked us if he could join us at our table we said, "Sure, please do." Our meals arrived earlier than theirs, so I said thanks to the Lord for the good food He had given us—not very formally I have to say. I didn't make it hard for them by announcing the fact that we were now going to say grace and get into a little huddle with Lorraine. However, my friend took notice because when his family's dinners arrived, he said something similar. It is amazing how God works with us if we give Him the praise He deserves. When the time comes to give glory to God the devil wants to make the situation embarrassing for Christians and non-Christians alike, but it need not be like that at all. There is a place for praising God in public and a way to do it. God has made Himself accessible to us through Jesus Christ; we have to make God accessible to others, to speak in a language they understand with concepts they can grasp.

9

The Shape of Praise

Barnabas was an encourager; that is what his name means. He took the newly converted Saul to the apostles when they were all suspicious of Saul. Barnabas let them know that Saul was genuine, and that they need not worry because Saul had seen the Lord. He praised and commended Saul to the leaders in Jerusalem by letting it be known that Saul had preached fearlessly in the name of Jesus, and the leaders listened to Barnabas (Acts 9:26–27).

To encourage people and stand up for people is an important thing to do. There is so much despair and fear in the world that people need to be encouraged. The devil has robbed many people of praise that they should have received. We don't praise people for doing wrong but when they have done well it ought to be acknowledged. People respond well to praise and are usually thankful for it. How many ways are there of letting it be known that someone has done a good thing? There are lots. We could write a letter telling them we were glad to hear of their accomplishment, send it to the local newspaper, or tell our friends, talk about it in an Internet chat room, or blog it somewhere. There is enough bad news in the world—how great it would be if we set ourselves a project of letting people know good news. I don't mean only telling people The Good News, but sharing good news from our community, good things people have done, or even stories from around the globe. And, of course, sharing good things that we hear God has done, for God is always at work.

We will often hear stories from the natural world around us and stories from people's lives that bear the mark of "God at work." We don't have to talk to people in a condescending artificial way, praise will come naturally when we rejoice and praise God for the good things that we hear about. Goodness is pushing back the devil's domain of darkness. We have to be careful not to think things unworthy of reporting to others unless they have some spiritual angle to them that we can use to preach to them. We have to be genuine and real. When we see that something good happening is a part of God's kingdom taking shape, we will be grateful that good things are happening because they are good. God *is* good! God's kingdom is goodness manifested. We are saved from being bad and doing bad things. If we could be good, we wouldn't need saving. Goodness counts; it is important.

If we make it a project to encourage and praise people it will soon become a way of life. When we talk to people it is good for us to encourage them in their achievements, maybe there aren't any other people around them who will do it. It is good for us to look for opportunities to praise people for efforts they have made towards any good pursuit. When someone dies there are often tributes given to the dead person at the funeral or memorial service. Why wait until the person is dead? Is it because we are afraid of them getting a big head? Perhaps people think it is better if we hang on until they die. Or is it because we regret not doing it while they were alive, and giving them some credit when they die is the next best thing? It is not our job to protect people from getting big heads; God is able to sort that out for them. It is remiss of us to fail to praise someone when the opportunity presents itself. I think it is fair to say that the balance of comments made in this world err on the side of destructive comments rather than constructive comments. So, there is plenty of room for praising someone. It is important that we do not become servile flatterers but let us not be afraid to give credit where credit is due to whomever deserves it.

Bibliography

Alighieri, Dante. *The Divine Comedy.* Translated and edited by Robin Kirkpatrick. Cambridge, England: Cambridge University Press, 2004.

Alighieri, Dante. *The Inferno.* The Divine Comedy. Translated and edited by Dorothy L. Sayers. United Kingdom: Penguin Books, 1949.

BBC News. "At a glance; Genetic code." No pages. Accessed June 27, 2007. Online: http://news.bbc.co.uk/1/hi/sci/tech/1165172.stml.

Blake, William. *Songs of innocence and of experience,* "The Tyger." Franklin Center, PA: Franklin Library, 1980.

Bible Presbyterian Church Online. Westminster Shorter Catechism. No pages. Accessed June 27, 2007. Online: http://www.shortercatechism.com/resources/wsc/wsc_001.html.

Briggs, Helen. BBC News. "Dispute over number of human genes: The human genome." No pages. Accessed June 27, 2007. Online: http://news.bbc.co.uk/1/hi/sci/tech/1426702.stml.

Chesterfield, *Lord Chesterfield's Letters.* Letter CXIII, May 17, O.S. 1750. Oxford, England: Oxford University Press, 1998.

Chesterton, G.K. *Philip Yancey Recommends: Orthodoxy, G. K. Chesterton.* London, England: Hodder and Stoughton Ltd, 1996.

Concise Oxford Dictionary. 9th ed. Oxford, England: Oxford University Press, 1995.

Contexo.info. "DNA Replication." No Pages. Accessed June 27, 2007. Online: http://www.contexoinfo/DNA_Basics/DNA%20Replication.html.

Ellicott, Charles John. *Bible Commentary for English Readers.* Vol I. London, England: EC Cassell and Company, not dated.

Frank, Jeffrey, and Diana Crone Frank. The Stories of Hans Christian Anderson: A New Translation from the Danish. New York, NY: Houghton Mifflin Books, 2003.

Franklin, Benjamin. "*Articles of Belief and Acts of Religion.*" Vol II, Part I. No pages. Accessed June 27, 2007. Online: http://www.historycarper.com/resources//twobf2/articles.html.

Keynes, John Maynard. "*Newton, the Man,*" In *Essays in Biography*. 2d ed. London, England: Rupert Hart-Davis, 1951.

Lewis, C.S. *Prayer: Letters to Malcolm*. Glasgow, Scotland: William Collins Sons & Ltd, 1964.

———. *The Great Divorce*. London, England: Geoffrey Bless Ltd, 1945.

———. *The Last Battle*. Glasgow, Scotland: William Collins Sons & Co Ltd, 1981.

———. *Reflections on the Psalms*. London, England: *Collins/Fount Publishers, 1977.*

Luke, Helen M. *The Laughter at the Heart of Things: Selected Essays by Helen M. Luke*. New York, NY: Parabola Books, 2001.

Muggeridge, Malcolm. *Conversion—A Spiritual Journey*. London, England: William Collins Sons & Co Ltd, 1988.

———. The National Review, "Nature is a Parable," December 24, 1982. New York.

Naeye, Robert. "Astronomy.com: Ask Astro." No pages. Accessed June 27, 2007. Online: http://www.astronomy.com/asy/default aspx?c=a&id=2196.

Newman, John Henry. *Apologia pro Vita Sua*. London, England: Longman, Green, Longman, Roberts, and Green, 1864.

———. *Meditations and Devotions*. Part 3. London, England: Longmans, Green, & Co., 1894.

Plato. *Great Dialogues of Plato: Complete Texts of the Republic, Apology, CritoPhaido, Ion, and Meno*. Vol I. Edited by E. H. Warmington, translated by W. H. D. Rouse. New York, NY: Signet Classics, 1999.

Rosenmuller, Ernest Friedrich Carl. *Scholia in Vetus Testamentum*. Partis Primae, Pentateuchus Annotatione. Vol S I–III. Leipzig, Germany: Jo. Ambros. Barthii, 1822.

Spurgeon, Charles Haddon. *Spurgeon's Devotional Bible*. Grand Rapids, MI: Baker Book House, 1964.

St. John, Patricia. *Harold St. John: A Portrait By His Daughter*. Shoals, IN: Kingsley Press, 2002.

The Watchtower, "Angels—How They Affect Us," January 15, 2006. Wallkill, NY: Watch Tower Bible and Tract Society of Pennsylvania.

Unger, Merrill F. *Unger's Bible Dictionary*. Chicago, IL: Moody Press, 1957.

Williams, Charles. *War in Heaven*. Back cover quote by Owen Barfield. Grand Rapids, MI: Wm. B. Eerdman's Publishing Company, 1990.

Willett, Edward. Edward Willett's Intergalactic Library: Science Columns: "DNA." No pages. Accessed June 27, 2007. Online: http://www.edwardwillett.com/Columns/dna.html.

www.ingramcontent.com/pod-product-compliance
Lightning Source LLC
Chambersburg PA
CBHW072010090426
42734CB00033B/2329